DRINK
DRANK
Drunk

BEN CANAIDER AND GREG DUNCAN POWELL

150 GREAT WINES
DRINK
DRANK
Drunk

2004 EDITION

RANDOM HOUSE AUSTRALIA

Random House Australia Pty Ltd
20 Alfred Street, Milsons Point, NSW 2061
http://www.randomhouse.com.au

Sydney   New York   Toronto
London   Auckland   Johannesburg

Published by Random House Australia, 2003

Copyright © Ben Canaider and Greg Duncan Powell, 2003

The Authors assert their moral rights to be identified as the Authors of this work.

All rights reserved. No part of this publication may be reproduced, stored in a retrieval system, or transmitted in any form or by any means, electronic, mechanical, photocopying, recording or otherwise, without the prior written permission of the publisher.

National Library of Australia
Cataloguing-in-Publication Entry

Canaider, Ben.
Drink, drank, drunk: 150 great wines.

2004 ed.
ISBN 1 74051 257 X

1. Wine and wine making – Australia. I. Powell, Greg Duncan.
II. Title.

641.220994

Cover and internal illustrations by Alex Rowland
Photography by Adrian Cook
Cover by Darian Causby/Highway 51 based on a design
by Greendot Design
Typeset by Letter Spaced
Printed and bound by Griffin Press, Netley, South Australia

10 9 8 7 6 5 4 3 2 1

To Fitzy,
For teaching us good fiscal housekeeping, correct rules of order, procedural prudence, due diligence, and the art of facsimile management . . . Fitzroy, here's to you.

CONTENTS

Introduction		viii
Chapter One	**WEEKDAY WINES**	1
Chapter Two	**SURVIVAL WINES**	37
Chapter Three	**ESTABLISHMENT WINES**	73
Chapter Four	**SENSUAL WINES**	105
Chapter Five	**UNKNOWN WINES**	135
Chapter Six	**UNPRONOUNCEABLE WINES**	165
Cellaring Versus Drinking		184
Epilogue		186
Glossary		188
Index		195

INTRODUCTION

Welcome to the third completely new, unabridged, totally independent, complete-with-passenger-airbag edition of *Drink Drank Drunk*. Once again we have tackled the three pantechnicons of product that turned up at Greg's remote South Coast property to pick out 150 wines that will fit into your life. Just sorting out all the grog was a full-time job; and given our dispositions towards labour, well, how should we put it? We quite like watching other people work . . .

As to the tastings, we gave our livers an absolute caning, but we did it. This year we had a brand-new tasting lab, and the productivity gains were enormous. Powering through the wine-juice we surprised even ourselves: quality was high and so plenty of reasonably fine wines were discarded as we whittled the short list down to the very best 150. That's what it says on the cover, so that's what you're going to get.

They're wines that fit into some part of human existence. If only more winemakers could get that message: over-wooded, overworked wines don't fit into anyone's life – or death. Statement wines full of unsubtlety might make an impact on an occasional or first-time wine drinker, but such wines are hard to enjoy all the way to the 750th millilitre – particularly if you like to drink wine for health reasons five days out of seven, with luncheon and your evening repast . . . At the end of the day, when everything is said and done, Australians make good wine, across the board, but that's not enough any more. Winemakers, we need a new wine revolution: chuck out the recipe books, stop benchmarking everything you make to Wolf Blass Black Label, and go for texture and balance and flavours more savoury than confectionary.

As for the consumers, there is one figure that continues to disappoint. Per capita wine consumption has remained static over the last three years at 20.4 litres. We still dream of an Australia where we drink 30 litres of wine per man, woman and child, per year, at least . . . We fervently believe that our country would be a much better place if more people drank more wine. So, if you are the least bit patriotic and know someone who doesn't drink wine, convert them – by force, if necessary. Just consider yourself part of the wine coalition of the good . . .

CHAPTER ONE
WEEKDAY WINES

Chapter One
WEEKDAY WINES

If you've been paying attention and purchased the last two vintages of *Drink Drank Drunk* you'll know something about Mandy and Rohan, our focus couple. Through their living, loving, laughing and learning about wine they've helped us all understand more about the topic of this book – drinking.

For those of you who've been doing that a bit too much and can't remember, or are new to *Drink Drank Drunk*, Rohan is an Aries, a bit of a control freak, a radiographer, and – at heart – an incurable romantic. He is also teetering on the brink of wine tosserdom. And had he not met Mandy one Tuesday night in a Thai takeaway, he may well have gone this way. Mandy works for a publishing house. She's vivacious, determined and passionate. She's an Aquarius . . . Rohan and Mandy moved in together; it's been more successful than not.

We find them now in the midst of another weekday night at home, Rohan having made dinner, Mandy having told him it was 'delicious darling', and half a bottle of wine having been consumed – although Ro tends to drink one more glass after dinner while he does the dishes . . .

As much as Mandy likes Ro's dinners, there are problems. As much as she likes the 15-dollar bottles of wine Rohan brings home to consume on a weeknight, she feels the money could be better spent – like on a holiday. Last winter she didn't go skiing at all – and it was a really good season. In the back of her mind also lurk health concerns: 'Shouldn't women drink half as much wine as men?' But none of these things are as important – or as worrying – as diet and money. It's not just that Rohan's putting on weight and denying it, it's also that a bottle of wine each weeknight comes to about $70 or $80 a week, which is more than $4000 a year, which is a pretty good skiing holiday . . .

Rohan sees things differently. Rohan always does. Rohan sees $4000 a year as being a ridiculously small amount of money to pay for the kind of nightly relaxation, pleasure, entertainment, and escape from irksomeness that wine provides. And this is not to forget all the associated – if slightly geeky – distractions that wine also brings. Rohan passes the time at work wondering what style, region or varietal he's going to drink that night.

But now, no longer insensitive to Mandy's concerns, Rohan has decided to cut down, and to remove bottled wine as a staple part of their diet. Rather than entrench his position and be stubborn about their weeknight wine consumption, he's prepared to give Mandy's approach a go. Wine on Wednesday night and the weekends only . . .

It goes all right for a while – for the first Monday and Tuesday night. It's not as if Rohan gets the shakes or anything, although Mandy does notice she doesn't sleep quite as well. By Wednesday night, after they've both had a particularly bad day at their respective 'careers', they open up their Wednesday-night bottle and it's gone before they've even cooked dinner. Almost unthinkingly they're on to a second. Mandy sleeps even more fitfully that night and has a worse day on Thursday than she did the day before. Rohan snores and has a nightmare about himself and Mandy drinking flagon sherry wrapped in brown paper bags. By the time the week finally grinds to a close, they're half-tanked at after-work drinks.

In the hungover fog of Saturday morning, there's a moment of clarity. In an attempt to follow a more puritanical fiscal and dietary line they've only managed to put their lives into a state of imbalance. Rather than enjoying a couple of glasses each night, they're wiping themselves out like a couple of sailors on shore leave whenever they're *allowed* to drink. The next week things are back to normal, although Ro did go for a jog . . .

WATER WHEEL Memsie Shiraz Malbec Cabernet Sauvignon 2002
$15

Here's a savoury, gravelly, screw-capped red wine redolent of the Australian bush – its flora, fauna and introduced pests. Kangaroo hides, rabbit burrows turning into gullies, blackberries choking ancient creeks, ant heaps, crushed rock freshly laid on fire tracks and wild fennel growing along railway sidings. The fruit flavours herein are fairly fresh and primary; they're sweet, generous and not too tricked-up. They give the wine depth and body before the tannins turn it towards home.

weekday winner

INCIDENTALS There are not enough wines like this. Solid, fresh, generous reds that haven't been made to within an inch of their lives, complete with a simple screw-cap top and a very affordable price. Again, it's all about blending. This wine contains two of Australia's red-wine staples: cabernet and shiraz – the regular Batman and Robin, the dynamic duo. They've got a new friend, too: malbec – the most underrated superhero going around.

BROWN BROTHERS Pinot Noir & Chardonnay
$18

This is another three-strike wine. It's been in *Drink Drank Drunk* in each of its three editions. We're wondering if wines in this guide should follow a sort of American presidential system – no fourth term. But that's crap; it's about merit, not megalomania. When this wine was lined up with its peers there was no competition. Brown Brothers could charge a lot for it, but don't tell them that. Cool-climate King Valley pinot and chardy grapes with lots of natural acidity are gently pressed and expertly *assemblaged* to produce this pale lemon-coloured, fluffy, yet taut, honeyed, creamed, appley and – at its core – pleasantly rich sparkling white wine. The bubbles are perfect.

INCIDENTALS Bottled sparkling wine is a remarkable weapon. In a country where it's illegal to buy even the most harmless firework, or even the most inoffensive and charming hand gun, anyone with $20 can purchase this light, hand-held anti-personnel weapon, or LHAPW. As the back label says: 'To open point bottle away from self and others.' It's an invitation, isn't it?

YARRA BURN Pinot Noir Chardonnay Pinot Meunier 2000
$24

Yes, we know that $24 is not really a weekday price-tag, but babies get born on weekdays and people get divorced on weekdays, so there's always something to celebrate. So spend some money! This wine is the real deal, besides: the classic three-grape champenois blend from a vintage year is bottle-fermented by Australia's finest sparkling winemaker – one of our favourites, Mr Fizzypants, Ed Carr. The colour shows some pinot of the noir and meunier variety; a little bit of bottle age; tart, wild strawberry; crème brulee; cushion-like bubbles; creamy texture and some very clever liqueuring – giving it richness atop a clean acid platform.

INCIDENTALS Just because it's a weekday doesn't mean you should be drinking 10-dollar rubbish fake bubbles. Otherwise why are you going to work? Celebration should be about blowing a bit of dough. As that great wine commentator Friedrich Nietzsche said, 'If you're celebrating on a 10-dollar wine the whole notion of that celebration must be called into question.'

BROWN BROTHERS Riesling 2002
$14

Walk your mind through a garden in flower. Lots of perennials, succulents, fruit trees in blossom, grassy swords, Arum lilies and some kid eating musk sticks. It's a very well-kept garden with one of those flasho, entirely hidden irrigation systems; the lawn's edges are always perfectly trimmed. The gardener works it every day – at the end of which he enjoys a long, tall glass of lemon cordial. He's a gentle octogenarian, as fit as a fiddle, and with all his own teeth.

INCIDENTALS It's no fanciful notion that we think of this wine as being fresh, yet, in a sprightly way, elderly; we reckon this sort of riesling would, if a mental disease made you do it, cellar well for five or so years.
The reason we think this is because of the wine's balance and, more importantly, its natural acidity and structure.

MIRANDA High Country Riesling 2002
$12

This is no fine, elegant riesling. It's well away from the austere end of the stick, but it's not clumsy either. Indeed, it's quite pretty. With a honeysuckle aroma so obvious you can almost taste it, the wine makes you smile on first sip rather than pull a face like a twisted sandshoe – the effect most serious rieslings have upon their victims at first sip. The honeysuckle carries on into the middle of your mouth when the King Valley's riesling grapes kick in. It finishes nicely. This is a gentle, soothing weekday beverage.

INCIDENTALS Regional reputations increasingly count for a lot in terms of Australian wine sales. As wine consumers (read drinkers) become more sophisticated (suck more wine) they begin to associate wine quality with regions. 'Oh cabernet, yes, Margaret River . . . It must be the Adelaide Hills for sauvignon blanc . . . Riesling? The Clare Valley of course . . .' Do these sound like axioms? Never live your life by axioms.

WYNNS Coonawarra Estate Riesling 2002
$16

When you buy a lemon from the stupidmarket, well, it looks like a lemon and smells like a lemon, but it always lacks a certain pungency. When you pick a lemon from your own tree, take it inside and zest it, the smell is both powerful and healthful. That's the sense we get from this unlikely Coonawarra riesling. The intensity and richness of the fruit swerves towards the tropical about halfway through your mouth, but then that healthful zestiness grabs the wheel again and you and the riesling are back on track, heading along the dead straight roads of Coonawarra. Indeed, this white never deviates from its path.

INCIDENTALS This bottle comes with another one of those neck-tag things. Take it off and open it out and you're presented with a triptych. But the contents aren't religious; or are they? The panels tell of the miracles of rieslings, of grapes to nectar, Stelvin caps, and wine's immortality when correctly cellared . . .

TAYLORS Clare Valley Riesling 2002
$16

If you're the sort of person who likes those weird Scandinavian sauna-and-snow routines you'll probably like the effect of this wine. Just as your palate registers the sweetness, everything gets turned on its head and this riesling then tastes of sea salt. You know, a bit like that taste in your mouth when you come out of the surf. The effect is similarly refreshing. In this sense, it's a two-in-one wine: pretty and sweet with musky honeysuckle and lemon-blossom notes followed by the flavour of the Pacific Ocean somewhere between Newcastle and Bega . . .

INCIDENTALS Riesling is fussy when it comes to climate. We don't mean where it's grown, but the temperature at which you serve it. Straight out of the fridge at six to eight degrees Celsius all you get is acid. Straight off the shelf at 18 degrees Celsius all you get is flabby fruit flavours. Somewhere between there, around about 12 to 14 degrees, is optimal.

TYRRELL'S LOST BLOCK Semillon 2002
$15

Here's a semillon that's pulling a few sick moves. It seems to charge out of the glass and assault your snout with a menagerie of different aromas: star jasmine, the shells little girls collect from the beach, preserved lemons, and lanolin-based face cream . . . It freaks you out a bit, but don't lose your nerve – drink some. The Lost Block rewards your courage with fantastic, citric, pure, clear textures and flavours. Indeed, once you've swallowed it you realise it's the kind of wine you can drink all day. And you can; it's only 10.5 per cent alcohol by volume.

INCIDENTALS Vintage 2002 was yet another terrible vintage in the Hunter Valley: it rained at the wrong times, was sunny when it shouldn't have been, and generally behaved in a way that wine regions shouldn't. Once again, semillon in the Hunter doesn't seem to be bothered; in fact, some of the better ones seem to come from the crappiest years . . .

POET'S CORNER Henry Lawson Semillon 2001
$18

With stinky smells that bring back memories of Clark Rubber above-ground pools and bloodshot eyes from bad chlorine additions, this wine's aromas provide an instant trip back to childhood. But it's not finished yet. Further sniffs reveal other childhood holidays. Low tides, estuaries where the river or lake meets the sea, molluscs on rocks, even a bit of sunburn cream . . . Minerals, salts, weak lemon cordial . . . No wonder it's perfect with the fish and chips you lived on in those same holidays.

INCIDENTALS One of the great things about semillon in Australia is its low alcohol level. This one, for instance, is only 10 per cent – which equates to almost six standard drinks. Compare this to your average 13.5 per cent Aussie chardonnay – eight standard drinks . . . That's why semillon's perfect for lunch – and fish and chips on holidays.

WEEKDAY WINES

MIRANDA High Country Sauvignon Blanc 2002
$12

The recipe for good sauvignon blanc is one of the most simple in the wine cookbook. So why is it that so many winemakers stuff it up? All you're looking for is crisp, dry fruit flavours, a bit of ping and a bit of zing. It's a naturally pungent and strident variety, so let it express itself. Fortunately that's what they've done here; from vineyard to bottle seems to have been a seamless transition. With a standard sauv blanc accent – a bit of guava, a bit of passionfruit, some kiwi fruit – it's a rich and succulent example. Because of this, it needs heavy chilling and a minimum of four people – but that's what it was designed for . . .

INCIDENTALS We need to be as stridently honest with you as sauvignon blanc is with its flavours. We don't like sauvignon blanc very much. Never have. Greg calls it mother-in-law wine. We probably hate it so much because it invariably lacks subtlety. The same reason we don't like Jim Carrey, Robin Williams, or Julia Roberts . . .

OYSTER BAY Marlborough Sauvignon Blanc 2002
$19

New Zealand sauvignon blanc has been a remarkable wine over the last 15 years or so; it has created its own market and taken the world by storm. How? Direct, uncomplicated, do-you-want-a-drink vigour. But it can be a bit over the top. Thankfully with this Oyster Bay white there's none of that jump-out-of-the-glass and punch-you-in-the-face flavour so prevalent in Marlborough sauv blancs; it's got intensity without stridency; indeed it has a very drinkable texture that reminds you of good rainwater – or is it seawater? It signs off with the faintest hint of mineral salt – or is it tears?

INCIDENTAL In fact, this is one of very few sauvignon blancs you could actually plan a meal over. Sauvignon blanc at the table can be like having dinner with a know-all. No one can get a word in and the dinner is ruined because this person won't shut up and let anyone else speak. Subtlety is not a sauvignon blanc strong point, but this one's got it.

KOONUNGA HILL Chardonnay 2002
$14

Another wine that is often heavily discounted, you could easily think this chardonnay was a lot more exotic than mere Hill de Koonunga. With judiciously integrated oak, a minerally tang, a grapefruity zing and, best of all, a degree of subtlety, it's a class act. The big company that makes this wine has finally got the message: more is not better. It's okay to back off the full-on flavours a bit in order to make a more weekday-friendly product. Serve it chilled though because as it warms up it's only questionable foible – high-ish alcohol – comes to the fore.

INCIDENTALS When a company like Penfolds spends millions of dollars frigging around trying to make a 'white Grange' (Yattarna), it might seem that this would hold no benefit for the normal wine drinker. Not true: the good news is the trickle-down effect because even a humble chardy like Koonunga Hill benefits. We recommend it – not Yattarna.

MIRANDA High Country Chardonnay 2002
$12

This is straight-up-and-down, no frills modern ocker chardy and we love it. There's enough rich tropical fruit at first whiff to give this wine an easy likeability – it helps to make it popular. But there are also some herbs and weeds freshly whipper-snipped, giving it a cleaner, greener kind of edge. The flavour is beefed up by evident alcohol (14% alc vol) and its ripe nectarine flavours are kept upright and on tippy-toes by some prickly acidity. Serve it well fridge-conditioned and, once again, remember: don't think, just drink.

INCIDENTALS Jim Miranda – the bloke who makes this product – is gentlemanly and polite in his advice about this wine's cellaring potential: 'You may wish to cellar this wine for a few years, but I prefer to enjoy it now . . .' What fantastic advice. If only more winemakers could let their children go free in this way . . .

WYNNS Coonawarra Chardonnay 2002
$16

Wynns Coonawarra Chardy straddles both the old and the new chardonnay styles: she's a classic Australian horsewoman with a good seat and she's adopting some of the more modern equestrian techniques. This is chardonnay furnished with opulent and fairly integrated oak, and by this we mean the resinous, bitter pencil-shaving types of smells and flavours that don't stick out too much. There are cashews, brazil-nut skins, and even a hint of hazelnut, plus distant echoes of rockmelon flesh and skin. Thankfully it finishes savoury rather than sweet.

INCIDENTALS If you've ever been to Coonawarra you'll understand why they crap on all the time about the red dirt – there is nothing else to talk about. It is arguably Australia's most boring, nondescript wine district, and if it wasn't for the vines decorating the flat un-undulating landscape, it would be a forgotten dot on Australia's map. Except for the cattle and the trees . . .

MOONDAH BROOK Chardonnay 2002
$14

At under 15 bucks you're getting some pretty fancy-pants, toasty-woasty, oak protocols here. So if you're into that stuff you're not going to believe your luck. There are all those smells of vanilla and cashews – the smells you get when you let chardonnay hang around in toasty oak barrels for a bit. Indeed, this is like a poor man's white burgundy. It's rich and has an after-blast of wood and chardonnay which you can exhale through your nostrils. This is really a head-filling wine. Good with strong-flavoured smoked fish, spicy food, or use it as a nasal decongestant.

INCIDENTALS If you're into wine, and you're into chardonnay, you'll know that Western Australian chardonnay is posh. This wine, given its price, shows you how much chardonnay we have flooding Australian rural landscapes. Forget the wine lake, if this goes on we'll soon be living in a post-vino-diluvian world.

GRAMP'S Barossa Chardonnay 2001
$16

Gramp's chardy is no befuddled old grandad. He's tasting fresh and surprisingly non-Germanic, which is odd given his Barossan origins. Wateriness is not normally a positive in wine, but in this case it is: as this wine registers its presence in your mouth there's an ethereal limpidity that has the effect of making you go 'ahhhh . . .' It's just an impression though; the chardonnay quickly kicks back in, finishing with a blend of resiny oak and minerally acidity. Good cheapish chardy.

INCIDENTALS Here's the rub: from a warm, generous, red-wine district like the Barossa you don't really expect clean, drinkable chardy like this one. You generally get big fat ones – they provide instant appeal, but soon tire your poor little palate. It seems the folks at Gramp's have got the message: 'Give us a drink, not a statement!'

DE BORTOLI Gulf Station Pinot Noir 2001
$15

As they say in sporting commentary, this wine had 'a big ask'. We tasted it directly after some very pricey, premium-end products. But it didn't suffer too badly, and that's a good sign. With pinot smells more at the strawberry/menthol end of the stick, and a meaner cherry taste that is long and lean, this wine nevertheless manages to punch above its weight. It's disciplined and well trained. There's a bit of soft, velvety texture just before the cheek-sucking tannins kick in at gulp's end. And if you've still got any doubts, well, look at the price again.

INCIDENTALS Gulf Station is a terrible name for a pinot. It sounds like a service station or an oil company. The name itself has some historical cachet in the Yarra Valley, but it's a second or third label and these basically end up being named after any local points of historical interest that are left. Why is it that wine has to be named after historical things anyway?

NINTH ISLAND Pinot Noir 2002
$23

Yes, 20-something dollars is a lot to pay on a school night, but if you want to drink pinot that isn't poison, what are you going to do? We tasted the cheapies and believe us, you don't want to put yourself through that. This is a young, budding pinot noir, with a rich, garnet colour and a brooding intensity. Over the next year this wine will have well and truly bloomed. It's hinting at its optimum display already: dark, rich liqueur cherries, a wet-chalk-and-limestone aroma, and a hint of something sanguine – blood on limestone. This is a tough pinot, but attractive nevertheless.

INCIDENTALS This is the 2002 version of this Ninth Island wine. The 2001 appeared in last year's guide, and the 2000 in the inaugural edition of *Drink Drank Drunk*. It differs each year to a great degree, yet it keeps coming up trumps. A lot of this is thanks to the work of Ninth Island's founder, Dr Andrew Pirie. His company was bought out by a Belgian tanning operation in 2002 and they asked him to leave. Go figure . . .

MOONDAH BROOK Merlot 2001
$16

If merlot is supposed to smell like violets, these ones are from a weird forest – maybe even a jungle. Indeed, they might be the flowers of one of those insect-eating plants, because the smell is quite fragrant and enticing, hinting at a suppleness and sweetness. But as soon as this wine gets you in its jaws, and before you know what's happening, its gastric juices are flowing . . . This merlot's tannins really go on the assault, turning this wine into a more sturdy and sausage-compatible red wine. This is an adults-only merlot. Don't buy it if you like de-sexed reds.

INCIDENTALS If we can be so bold, we'd like to congratulate the person who redesigned the Moondah Brook label. Moondah Brook has been around longer than a lot of the people reading this book. The label needed an update – not a big change, just a bit of tweaking. Whoever did the tweaking has a good eye for colour and would probably be a famous artist if they were let out of the design department. Some people are afraid of their dreams . . .

SHADOW'S RUN Shiraz Cabernet Sauvignon 2001
$12

'An adequate luncheon wine', as Ben's Uncle Keith said while helping himself once more to this screw-capped product. He'd made his standard house pasta: Spaghetti à la Keith, its peppery pesto and smoky bacon flavours combining well with the wine's richness, uncomplicated berry flavours, faint gravel texture, and attractively savoury and sour finish. There's plenty of oomph, McLaren Vale chocolate, and a touch of Langhorne Creek depth, but it's all kept in its kennel by cleansing acidity. You can drink a lot of this red – and Uncle Keith did . . .

INCIDENTALS While he likes the wine, Uncle Keith hates border collies. As you can see from the bottle's label, Shadow is a BC. 'Idiot, stupid dawgs,' says Keith. 'They'll chase anything. Border collie? More like borderline! Those dogs are mentally unhinged.' Of course, Uncle Keith's attitude towards border collies is the same as his attitude towards all 'dawgs'. It's just another manifestation of his loveable but extreme temperament. Don't get him started on 'loony left-wing ideologues' . . .

D'ARENBERG The Stump Jump Grenache Shiraz Mourvèdre 2001
$12

This is weekday medicine. It's easy on the purse (or wallet), easy on the palate, and – potentially – easy on whatever's on your plate. It will cure loads of weekday ailments, such as Want-To Kill-Everyone-itis, and the How-Many-Days-Till-The-Weekend (or HMDTW) virus. It soothes and eases the aches and pains that make up much of our workaday lives. Easy to imbibe, there's a hint of camphored mulberry and spiced, gently stewed cherries; it's also rich and not too rough on the throat. It leaves without slamming the door, so to speak. Just a word of warning: If pain persists quit your job . . .

INCIDENTALS Life imitates art – it's a cliché, but it just keeps on repeating itself . . . a bit like history . . . This wine is named after the stump jump plough invented in South Australia and invaluable in the heavily timbered Australia, pre D8 bulldozers. McLaren Vale (where this wine comes from) is now so full of gnarly, untrellised bush vines (which this wine is made from) that if the land had to be re-cleared, the stump jump – or its modern equivalent – would once again have to be called into service.

MAD FISH Western Australia Premium Red 2001
$17

The Mad Fish undersells itself slightly. Modestly calling itself a Western Australian Premium Red, it's actually a bit better than that. It's a cab sav/merlot/cab franc blend that has quite a bit of grip – rock climbers could use it for practice. Lying just below this textured rough surface is a pool of plum juice. This is where the luxury is. Alongside that you'll find a touch of V8 vegetable juice – no doubt from the cabernet sauvignon – but mostly this wine is all about grip. It hangs on and dries out your mouth. Once again, if you want to taste it at its best, serve with meat.

INCIDENTALS Mad fish? What upsets fish? Apparently cod get cranky when they hear the Max Bygraves song 'Tulips from Amsterdam'; sturgeon are said to detest ABBA; apparently tuna react very badly to dolphin nets; and that shark in *Jaws* must have really hated the theme music. He ate people whenever they played it.

YALUMBA Bush Vine Grenache 2000
$15

Grenache is, for most part, a pretty simple sort of wine – the red grape-variety equivalent of a romantic comedy. But this one's different. For instance, it's already three years old, which gives it a few different flavours that it didn't have when it was a bairn. The simple raspberry notes have become a little more complex: some exotic spiced meats, and some headiness; liqueur chocolates, and cold, dark cupboard smells which add to its brooding mystery. Yet, paradoxically, it travels through the mouth with ease and grace, and finishes in a clean and linear manner. Try it with mild curry.

INCIDENTALS This wine's called Bush Vine grenache. What does that mean? You don't find grenache in the Australian bush. No, the bush vine is a wine plant that goes to an alternative, 'community' school – rather than a posh, private one. There's no discipline, no trellising, no careful rows of robotic wine plants all doing what they're told. There's not too much irrigation either, and that's what makes it good.

HOUGHTON Rockwall Cabernet Sauvignon 2001
$13

For a big-company wine there's plenty of personality here. It's as if it's been made by a slightly crazed, curly-haired Italian–Australian with a penchant for wine character as opposed to banal consistency. This is no wine robot. That's why it smells a bit out here: fresh silage, rabbit skins, home-pickled olives, a truckload of bay leaves, a bit of sage leaf wrapped around prosciutto. The flavours are textural and plush, but with a salty and savoury edge. It makes for a very enjoyable drink – and an absolute winner with your bunny stew.

INCIDENTALS Wines like this one – that is, wines that are a little bit weird – are like fresh fruit: consume them sooner rather than later. The very qualities that send this wine a bit out there can, if left alone with the wine for a few years, return to bite its bum – and yours.

WYNNS Coonawarra Shiraz 2001
$16

This particular example of Australian shiraz could be the commercial benchmark. It is line and length Aussie red; you can tick off the shiraz inspector's checklist: pepper, tick; earth, tick; spice, tick; a range of berries (blue and black), tick, tick; dry and dusty oak, tick; plums, tick . . . In fact, it is better than that, because on those points where the wine could go off the rails (like the oak one), it hangs on, showing integration and balance. But maybe that's a problem? Is it too well behaved? Well, some weeknights you want that; you don't want another fight with a wine over dinner . . .

INCIDENTALS Mocha. Football and cricket watchers will know of the term to 'put the mocha' on another player. This phrase was born in South Australia in the 1880s when rival full-forwards would get each other blind on heavily wooded red wine the night before the game. True story. (It has since entered back-label language – 'mocha characters'.)

ROSEMOUNT Hill of Gold Mudgee Shiraz 2001
$19

Hill of Gold may be a poxy name, but it's the ideal tonic after a hard day at your workstation. It provides everything you require, having stripped off the work attire and settled in for the 12 to 14 hours that are yours before work starts again: alcohol (14.5 per cent of it, in fact), more-ish blackberry aromas and flavour, and enough earthy grip and backbone to stand up to the fantastic meal you have in your mind but probably won't bother to prepare. Still, there's plenty of solid red wine here to console you as you eat your takeaway and dream of escape . . .

INCIDENTALS Mudgee, north-west of Sydney, is a wine region that finds it virtually impossible to produce fine, elegant reds. Thankfully this means that big companies like Rosemount can't ferment all the character out of their Mudgee products. Wines like this Hill of Gold are the proof.

KNAPPSTEIN Clare Valley Shiraz 2001
$20

This is what Clare Valley shiraz is about – and it's only $20. With shedloads of fragrantly timbered plush berry smells and then a 6-foot-4-inch, 16-stone whack of classic Clare tannins, you are left in no doubt as to what you're getting. Don't be in a nancy-boy mood when you pull the cork on this one. It will handle fatty foods very well too; the acidity at the end of the wine carries all before it, cleaning out the highways and byways of your mouth and getting everything ready for more food and wine. A complete experience.

INCIDENTALS Yet again, we like this winemaker's cheaper wines rather than his expensive ones. Why do they do what they do with the expensive wines? It costs them more; it costs us more; it ultimately costs the world more. Why can't we have more affordable and drinkable red wine?

TAYLORS Shiraz 2001
$15

We have a theory to explain this wine's quality: while other wines from this outfit have disappointed this year, this relatively simple shiraz escaped the oak punishment its brothers and sisters had to endure. It was also released from the wine factory with a relatively affordable price-tag. Good news for weekday drinkers: they get big, round and soft shiraz fruit, full of ripe blueberry and blackberry; they get a hint of chocolate (but thankfully that's all – too much chocolate makes you sick); and they also get sweetness balanced by a stony, minerally finish. Good, very good red plonk indeed.

INCIDENTALS At the 15-dollar mark it is a good idea to choose reds from regions like the Clare Valley, in South Australia. There are plenty of old vines around; plenty of winemaking and grape growing expertise; and – despite all that – no overblown, silly reputation. This is not quite the ego region that some other spots in SA are . . .

MITCHELTON Blackwood Park Cabernet Sauvignon 2000
$17

Grape varieties are sometimes hard to identify. Even the most smarty-pants wine bores can mistake cabernet and shiraz. There'd be no mistaking Blackwood Park. It's textbook, central Victorian, varietal cabernet sauvignon. Suck it and see. Cassis with a green edge, eucalyptus on a hot day, a hint of iron-ore, ironbark, tightly wound minerally atoms of tannin that at the end of your mouth all come together to form a textural final assault. The only thing that will defend you against this wine is a big rare juicy steak, or possibly a sausage.

INCIDENTALS Sausages are a little-known, and little-used, form of personal defence. For centuries highly trained wine warriors have armed themselves with a sausage, be it bratwurst, chorizo, or supermarket BBQ before they have fought any duel involving cabernet sauvignon . . .

TAHBILK Cabernet Sauvignon 2000
$19

Berried, distantly camphor-chested, rich and very friendly – and with structure and tannins to match which save this wine from the mundane. They're old-fashioned and happily rustic tannins – open and grainy as opposed to oak-derived and toxic. Plums are lying around on the ground underneath the tree; there are autumn leaves bespeckled by late-afternoon sun; the earth is still faintly fertile . . . The edges of this Tahbilk red are squared off, and it goes through your mouth that way too – not tapered, but solid. Reassuring. Drink it young and never apologise for it.

INCIDENTALS *Drink Drank Drunk* recidivists will keenly remember that tannins are the gruff textural bits in red wine – just like sucking on a tea bag. Tannins come from three sources. There is grape tannin – they're natural and good; there are oak tannins from barrels – they can be overdone and toxic; and then there are evil artificial tannins that come out of a packet – and back labels never mention them.

WATER WHEEL Bendigo Shiraz 2001
$18

Greg reckons that if God made him choose only one wine to drink for the rest of his life he'd choose this one. Why? Well there's so much going on. It's never boring and it never berates. On the one hand it has that old-fashioned Australian red-wine honesty and sustenance. The big, fat, black-cherry fruit flavours are deep and warm; the tannins are plentiful and drying; there's an easy, laconic generosity. Yet on top of all this there comes some refinement, quality and class. It is, according to Greg, a very difficult wine to spit out . . . He drank most of it with dinner – by himself.

INCIDENTALS If cattle didn't exist, or we were all Hindus, this wine wouldn't be as interesting. That's because it is ideally suited to the consumption of beef. Tasty cuts such as rump or porterhouse, standing rib roasts, char-grilled T-bone, but not beef fillet. You need a boring wine for beef fillet because it's so boring itself.

# CHAPTER TWO
SURVIVAL WINES

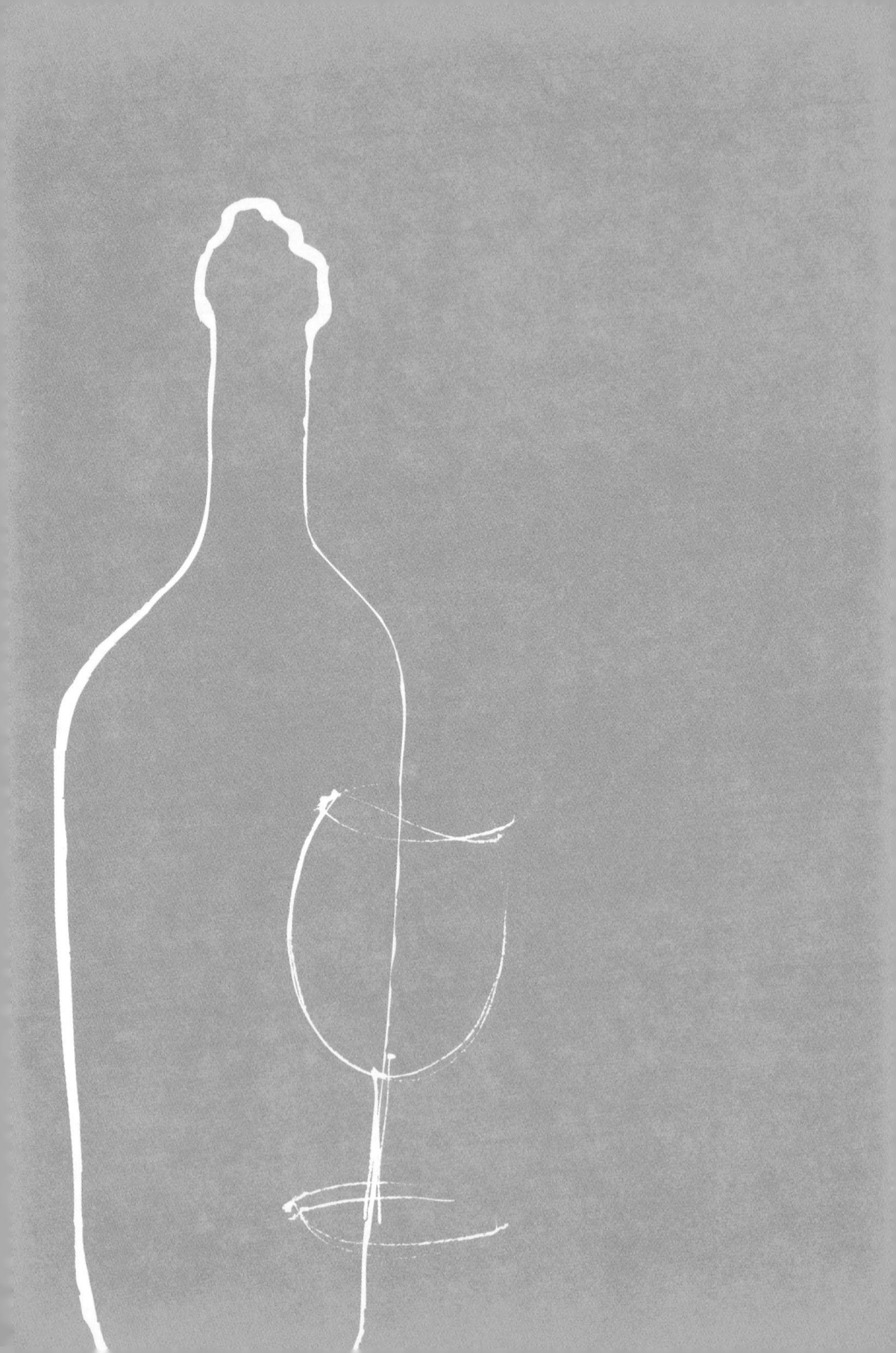

Chapter Two
SURVIVAL WINES

Mandy has a great job. Or she used to. She worked for a minor publishing house managing two specialist magazines – *Urban Lifestyle Now* and *Australian Women's Rugby*. But both failed to get advertising; they folded – and so did Mandy's job. It was nothing to do with Mandy. She knows this and besides, she's never been the sort of woman to link her self-esteem to her job anyway – that's a disaster. Nevertheless she's proud and she's pissed off. It's not so much the job but the lack of income. Rohan, because he loves her so much, is happy to pay for everything until Mandy finds a new workstation. Yet Mandy's pride . . .

And there's another little problem. No, she's not pregnant. Worse. Rohan failed to get his promotion. He's a bit depressed: it looks like another two years of lubricating the ultrasound machine and staring at people's innards via the fuzzy, pixilated images on the computer screen.

Bad luck comes in threes. Mandy's old Barina got bingled as well. So it's time for some serious budgeting. Dollars are being lopped off every outgoing. No expenditure is safe, not even wine.

Mandy and Rohan, welcome to the world of casks.

Australians, as 101 per cent of the readers of this book will know, invented casks. The archetypal cask is a four-litre bladder pack. Then there emerged the two-litre cask, and then the three-litre 'premium' cask, now euphemistically known as the 'convenience pack'. Rohan and Mandy try them all. They do everything to convince themselves that they're drinking fine wine. They decant the cask red into crystal, drink it out of Rohan's best Riedel's and even try to cook things that go with cask wine – baked beans, macaroni cheese and such. But nothing works. They find themselves drinking more and more in their search for satisfaction. Rohan has even tried blending a bit of cask port with the red to give it some more grunt. The result was a terrible hangover. Eventually they find a couple of brands they don't mind.

Little did Mandy and Rohan know that they were drinking some of the best-quality cask wine in yonks. Bad as their luck had been, they had been fortunate enough to be poor at a time when cask wine was drinkable. There are so many vines in the ground and so much bulk wine in storage that better quality wine has eventually trickled down to the cask at the bottom of the wine-quality pyramid. Yet it's still a hit-and-miss affair. If you're used to drinking bottled wine you'll miss it. It's rare you'll find a cask that measures up, and even when they fell upon a decent cask, Mandy and Rohan still missed the variety of bottled wine.

Eventually the planets moved, Aquarius came under the influence of Mars, and Mandy and Rohan's luck changed. One big company, let's call them Northcorp, paid a super-executive megabucks to rebadge, redistribute and re-*everything* an otherwise successful range of wines. It was a major fuck-up. He got sacked – sorry: he resigned and received a handsome payout. The legacy of his tenure was the firesale and heavy discounting of some otherwise fine wine.

Mandy first noticed the effects of this corporate shakeout as she was walking to her Yogalates class. A red that she could have sworn she saw Rohan pay $20 for when they were rich was being sold for $10.99. She bought it. Other re-*everything*ed Northcorp wines soon turn up in the firesale – 15-dollar products that went for $8, 10-dollar products that went for $6. Mandy finds them all and takes them home to a delighted Rohan.

Addicted to this new pastime, Mandy decides to delay getting the Barina's bingle bashed out and spend her Centrelink cheque and her spare time hunting down wine bargains. Scouring the financial pages, she sniffs out mergers and meltdowns in wine companies almost before they happen.

She's the first at the biggest liquor chains as the corporate casualties arrive with their new price-tags.

Mandy derives a lot of satisfaction from this new extreme sport, and it's been the sort of experience that has brought Rohan and her closer together. It's funny how everything balances out: three weeks later she finds herself the deputy editor of *Celebrity Now* magazine on a very good package, and Mandy and Rohan are well and truly back on the bottles again . . .

PENFOLDS Rawson's Retreat Cabernet Sauvignon 2002
$10

survival winner

You could have a lot of fun with this wine, not least because it's a pretty good drink and has 14 per cent alcohol by volume. It could also fool a lot of wine tossers – in three ways. It tastes more expensive than it is; it has a lot of the varietal characteristics of full-bodied cool-climate shiraz; and, although it tastes as if nothing is missing, this is a wine produced without any oak. There are blackberries (with plenty of seeds in them), cassis and pepper. See what we mean about cool-climate shiraz? It's a big mouthful of wine and it finishes firmly – thanks to the fact it's cab sav.

INCIDENTALS Big-company cheap red wine with no oak? What's going on? Big companies have realised that many of their cheap wines are ruined by the addition of crappy, budget oak products. Quite literally they throw oak chips or oak sawdust into the wine. No wonder the effect is invariably shithouse. This wine has particularly good fruit, and hats off to Penfolds for not spoiling it.

ORLANDO Trilogy Cuvée Brut
$13

What saves this survival product from going down the sink (like the many it was tested with in our brand-new tasting lab) is its structure. Most cheap sparklers smell pretty shithouse and taste even worse: sulphur, juicy fruits, boiled lollies, sugar . . . Trilogy – called that because it's got the three main champenoise grape varieties – pinot noir, chardonnay, pinot meunier – has a bit more going on. It's bound together, balanced with ripe apple flavours that are polished and smooth. And the wine's best asset – its structure – is taut enough to keep the wine on track from lips to throat. And it has that weird smell: half cider, half malt whisky . . .

INCIDENTALS There are some anomalies in Orlando. It is a company in which they wear synthetic shirts and Hush Puppies and perversely (given the couture) is owned by a French company, Pernod Ricard. It seems that although the French company is quite happy to take the profits of Orlando it doesn't return the favour by offering the employees any fashion or grooming budgets . . .

JACOB'S CREEK Riesling 2002
$10

Jacob's Creek riesling is the Social Security office of the wine world. The safety net when you're down and out. This wine is the proverbial friendly face at the counter, ever so ready and happy to hand you an emergency-relief-funds cheque . . . Once you get it, go straight next door and buy a few bottles of this. For a cheapo riesling it lifts you to a truly socially secure place, complete with full employment. Here the air is full with the smells of honeysuckle, lime trees, swimming pools, wandering Jew . . . Tastes are rich but always saved by sophisticated acidic edge.

INCIDENTALS If you look at the other photographs of rieslings in this book, you'll notice that those bottles invariably conform to one particular style and shape – tall, thin, sloping-shouldered jobs known as the riesling bottle. So anal and fixated with unimportant ephemera do wine tossers become that they look askance at riesling not bottled thus. We do. Do you too?

LINDEMANS Bin 75 Riesling 2002
$9

If you're looking for cheap bottled white wine and you're not particularly thrilled with wood-chipped chardonnay, flabby verdelho, or that weapon of mass destruction, sauvignon blanc – then give this Bin 75 a go. But aren't rieslings sweet? And if they're not sweet, then aren't they sharp and hurtful? Yes and yes, and no and no. We tasted this riesling at 8.37 am on a Saturday morning and we didn't mind it. Its flavours sit somewhere below the hardcore and strident acidity of many Australian rieslings. Effeminate, mutedly citric, a touch of hair-oil weight without any flab, and a small posy of flowers . . . It's quite cute really but, like all rieslings, serving temperature is critical. This one needs heavy chill.

INCIDENTALS One of the more ridiculous things to emerge from the sick and warped minds of wine marketers lately is neck tags on bottles. Standing out on the bottle-shop shelves is half the battle, we know; but so many bottles now wear this neck-tag jewellery it's the ones without it that might soon stand out.

LEASINGHAM Bastion Clare Valley Riesling 2002
$13

This wine is well named. It is a bastion, a bulwark against sweetened-up and confused cheap riesling. We believe that if you shop around you'll find this big-company white at a much lower price than its RRP. What you get here is pure Clare Valley riesling citric minerality and great length. If this wine were a woman she'd be fairly leggy. There's a fragrance of frangipani, lime blossom and gardenia; in the glass it is pert and star-bright. We really like it.

INCIDENTALS This is an example of what a really good vintage can do to a fairly inexpensive wine. The year 2002 in the Clare Valley was one that put smiles on the dials of all the region's riesling makers; it has made this inaugural Bastion riesling a much better drink than rieslings three times the price from other regions. Bastion has come out firing.

TYRRELL'S Old Winery Semillon Hunter Valley 2002
$12

Here's a pert yet viscous-looking Hunter Valley semillon – and remember the Hunter Valley is all about semillon – that delivers all you want from this fantastic, versatile and long-haul white: good things like lemon, lemon trees, salt licks; weird things like lanolin, grapefruit peel, paspalum; and really odd things such as Nylex hose, pool liners, battery acid . . . What a fantastic ethereal drink – forget mineral water. And you get all of these things in one 750-ml package. It's a wine that makes you think of killing molluscs and eating them very fresh.

INCIDENTALS Vintage 2002 will be memorable only because it was so bad. We tasted plenty of ponceforth Hunter semillons from this year – most of them tasted like expensive 30-dollar slightly acidulated water. We are again amazed that our very good friends at Tyrrell's can make a semillon like this in such a year for such a price.

ROSEMOUNT Diamond Label Semillon 2002
$13

This wine is quite an achievement. In fact, we were truly startled at the price given the quality. At first it smells like a once verdant lucerne paddock now drought-afflicted; you take another deeper sniff and that lush greenery comes into sharper focus. The paradoxical nature continues once it gets past your lips – it's both rich and drying. The flavour in your mouth seems really intense, but once swallowed dissipates leaving a dry, open aftertaste. Lemon, gooseberry, green apple and weeds . . . As we said, it's quite an achievement . . .

INCIDENTALS What would you eat with a wine like this? We're in survival mode, and it is one of the very few wines that can handle that staple of survival foods: soup. Especially won ton soup, chicken noodle soup, fishball soup, matzo ball soup, pumpkin soup. And it wouldn't be too bad with spicy noodle dishes either. Semillon is very versatile when it comes to Thai and Nonya foods.

JACOB'S CREEK Semillon Sauvignon Blanc 2002
$8

Note the title of this wine: it is a sem/sauv blanc – not the other way around. And that is its saving grace. At this price point, structure is one of the first things to be sacrificed. Not here. The semillon provides structure as well as flavours of citrus, dried grass, lemon trees, and a zippy texture as it cuts a swathe through your salivating mouth – like a mower with brand-new blades powering through a spring lawn. The sauvignon blanc kicks in with some richer, tropical fruits, but thankfully it's just a cameo.

INCIDENTALS *Drink Drank Drunk* recidivists will know how much delight we find in back-label verbiage. Quote – 'This dry white wine style is ideally suited to Australia's alfresco lifestyle.' – close quote. Do you actually know anyone who would say to you, over lunch, 'Isn't this wine ideally suited to our alfresco lifestyle?' Again, we advise that if they do, drop them . . .

SURVIVAL WINES | 49

HOUGHTON Semillon Sauvignon Blanc 2002
$12

Less is more with sem/sauv blanc blends. You want flavour but not too much; you want white wine's lick of subtle alcohol, but not so much that you think you're drinking vodka. This one smells of passionfruits just sliced open, with that same acid piquancy. The body of the wine is quite light which makes it easy to drink, and rather than being zingy or zesty – as you'd expect from a lot of these young blends – the flavours intensify, pulling into really sharp focus right at the end of the mouthful. Just as salty as it is fruity, it is the perfect wine to sip – well chilled – while you're significant other whippersnips those unruly bits of the backyard.

INCIDENTALS All wine styles have a certain role: cabernet is serious and needs lamb, shiraz is earthy and spicy and likes almost any meat, chardonnay has more body and texture and is well suited to similarly constructed fish, verdelho is for killing weeds (apply directly wearing safety gloves and goggles), and sem/sauvs are for afternoon sipping.

HAZARD HILL Semillon Sauvignon Blanc 2002
$12

Don't be put off by the cheap price – this wine tastes much more expensive than its RRP suggests. With high-end grapefruit, lemon zest and lychee Pez smells, the alcohol-inspired rich and syrupy texture reminds us of the juice you find in a can of tinned apricots. Thank goodness the wine finishes very cleanly and crisply with a minerally acidity, although the aftertaste has a distant ring of that tinned syrup. Our very serious advice to anyone tackling this 12-dollar tonic is to refrigerate it heavily and consume within hours of purchase.

INCIDENTALS Much of the appeal, structure, flavour and uninhibiting power of this sem/sauv comes from its level of alcohol: turbo-charged at 14 per cent. Alcohol helps to track flavour in wine – like the rails that guide a train. It makes wine easier to taste (or should that read less subtle?). High alcohol also adds to body and texture – both in wines and sometimes in two mutually attracted drinkers . . .

HOUGHTON White Burgundy 2002
$12

White burgundy this is not, but who cares; it's a reasonably full and faintly rich, dryish white custom-made for fusion takeaway, inoffensiveness, and liquor-store discounting. It's Granny Smith apples and William pears that have been sweetened up a bit, as if vitamised in a food processor with a bit of caster sugar. They're still fresh and lively and quite crisp, and they weren't peeled before they were liquidised. They were, however, cored. For this wine has that little bit of bite from the fruit skin; this saves it from being one of those things that never finish – like Elton John's syrupy career.

INCIDENTALS There's an old winemaking story that goes something like this: A winemaker lay dying in his bed; his sons all gathered around. 'Sons, you know all those vines out behind the apple and pear orchards at the front of the farm?' he whispered feebly. 'Yes Dad, we know about all those grapes', they replied. 'You can make wine out of those grapes too . . .'

ENCOUNTER BAY Classic Dry White 2001
$12

Here's a wine that can really wake you up, just the sort of pert, zesty white to help you deal with the modern survival diet: stir-fry, stir-fry, and stir-fry . . . Oh, and bad TV, and videos you've seen before, and the four walls of your bedsit. With a mid-spring whiff of well-watered honeysuckle, some spice, some rich and buttery lemon and a blast of citric acidity so sharp it breaks the seals on the saliva glands, this wine helps you break on through to the other side. It'll go magnificently with yet another stir-fry, and the umpteenth viewing of *Sleepless in Seattle*.

INCIDENTALS Little-known wine fact #326. Acidic white wine, in many respects, is a solvent. Take two teaspoons of this Encounter Bay white-wine product, and, using a needleless syringe, squirt the wine into the aforementioned videotape. Rotate the tape three times and all traces of Meg and Tom will be erased. You are free; no more video. Ring a friend, or have an early night . . .

TAHBILK Marsanne 2002
$12

The first thing to note about Tahbilk Marsanne is that it's often discounted below $10, hence its inclusion in this chapter. With some keen yet rich grapefruity and lemon notes, the smell reminds us of effervescent vitamin C tablets, saltiness and Fruit Tingles. Nettles lurk in the background, as does some mild steel – so it's well balanced. Inside your mouth there's wham-bam fruit-salad flavour; it quickly disappears leaving a minerally, long fresh aftertaste. Ripe lemons, fresh grapes . . . What's it matter what grape a wine is made from when it's as drinkable as this?

INCIDENTALS Australia's most underrated, worthwhile and affordable white could just be Tahbilk Marsanne. Who cares that the grape variety is one of the rarest in Australia, that it comes from France's pretty Rhône Valley, that it has an ability to cellar (which titillates the wine cognoscenti), or that it's blah, blah, blah . . . Just drink it, enjoy it and shut up.

PENFOLDS Rawson's Retreat Semillon Chardonnay 2002
$10

This has got to be one of the best-value whites in this chapter – and that's saying a lot. For only a tenner you're getting a pretty handily put together product. True, it was made in massive stainless steel tanks, and wasn't finessed by the gentle hand of some worried winemaker. But working the control panel of a giant winery takes skill too. It's got lanolin, the sort of lemon-and-herb seasoning you rub over chicken, a whiff of rockmelon skin, and richness that dries out into a broad texture, filling your whole mouth. It's good stuff and we reckon it would be great with that same lemon-and-herb chicken.

INCIDENTALS What was Rawson retreating from? It goes back to Gallipoli. As the boats landed on the beach that fateful morning, everyone got out and got shot – except Rawson. Halfway to shore, he remembered he had left his dry white wine back on the boat. Going to war was fine. But going to war without wine was unacceptable.

HOUGHTON Chardonnay 2002
$12

We think this chardonnay smells a bit like a lemon tree – one that's just been sprayed with a mixture of pyrethrum and white oil: it's got scale . . . But that's not a criticism. It doesn't smell of cheap woodchips and tinned tropical fruit – for which we're very thankful. There *are* hints of tropical fruit, but it's fresh tropical fruit – all of which has been carefully chosen at the market and then lovingly assembled at home. There's nothing tinned about it. Sharp acidity helps this wine to pierce the inner sanctum that is your fish-and-chip-flavoured mouth.

INCIDENTALS We invite you to compare this chardonnay with the William Fevre Petit Chablis on page 174. There really is no comparison. They are two entirely different things. We prefer to drink more of the latter but it is about three times the price. However, we can still drink a few glasses of this and that's what it's designed for – careless drinking for the poor and needy.

DE BORTOLI Windy Peak Pinot Noir 2001
$12

This is a remarkable wine given the price. High volume, affordable, varietal, and drinkable pinot noir – that's almost impossible. How have they done it? First, there's the signature garnet and slightly confused colour typical of pinot; then some considerable depth follows with rich, deep fruit reminiscent of old, withered cherries underscored by a trace of menthol and the smell of thawing rump steak. Wood-char and more cherries provide the substance as you drink; and its 12-dollar price-tag only raises its head if you care to concentrate on the tannins at the back of your mouth – they're more coarse than silky, but don't really detract from the overall package.

INCIDENTALS The back label of this fine pinot product brags about cold maceration, whole bunch addition and warm fermentation, and minimal handling and filtration. These are all bits of winemaking lore where pinot-making is concerned. In laundry terms the wine had a prewash soak on a short warm-water cycle. No fabric softener was used.

SURVIVAL WINES

JACOB'S CREEK Grenache Shiraz 2002
$10

Forget the grenache/shiraz bit. This is full-bodied Australian beaujolais and can be utilised for exactly the same sorts of thoughtless drinking occasions – casual lunches, big parties, late-morning drinks, picnics (or as the French say, *le pique-nique*), work functions, et cetera. It smells of half-chewed Redskin lollies on wet concrete. This confectionary element is thankfully trodden on by a bit of cherry and plum and some fairly hefty alcohol, plus some drying tannins. There's actually a fair bit going on, and to get the same thing in a Beaujolais you'd be paying three times this price.

INCIDENTALS This simple red is best not drunk at room temperature (unless your room is 12 degrees Celsius). In warmer conditions it performs at its best after 20 minutes to half an hour in the fridge. Alternatively, it is ideally priced and constructed to turn into a sangria . . . Yes, it is okay to do such things to wine . . .

ROSEMOUNT ESTATE Grenache Shiraz 2002
$11

This wine recommends itself not as an individual but rather as one amongst its peers. In the team of grenache/shiraz reds (the 2nds) Rosemount is a bit of a star. He is far more skilful than the rest of the team but he wouldn't want to try to play in the 1sts or, for that matter, in a better league. This is good, widely available, blended red, barbecue product. You get grenache's fruit, colour and alcohol; you get shiraz's earth, spice and grunt, and a few silky moves on the palate. An honest player but no star.

INCIDENTALS Buying cheap wine for parties. You've got a squillion people coming around for your better half's/mother's/nephew's/old friend from overseas/dog's birthday party . . . You want to buy a case of red to help soak up the barbecue. It has to have alcohol in it and be drinkable. This is the wine. Cater with two bottles a head and it'll be the best party ever . . .

SURVIVAL WINES

PETER LEHMANN Barossa Shiraz Grenache 2002
$12

The ideal luncheon red for those of us on a budget. Australia has too few of such wines and the ones it has are in this book. This Peter Lehmann product is one of the best. The colour is really good: a dark magenta. The smells and tastes make you think of an angry red jube lolly on alcohol – raspberry, cassis, shiraz . . . Imagine Angry Anderson as a wine . . . If there is any oak in this wine it is hiding, which is a good thing. Wood at luncheon disables digestion. The gruffness at mouth's end lets you know you're drinking red, and maybe the only gripe is the level of alcohol; but that will help sort the afternoon out even more effectively . . .

INCIDENTALS As you may have guessed, one of our core brand values is luncheon. We are not talking about foccacia or any of that other non-food, but sit-down luncheon with a knife and fork. We also believe that wine should be drunk at lunch. Every day. It aids productivity, in an inverse sort of way: with some wine in you, you do fewer busy, stupid activities at your workstation in the afternoon; as a result the world is a less-crowded, clamoured place. Balance. Peace. Drink wine at lunchtime!

LINDEMANS Cawarra Merlot 2002
$7

It's weird isn't it that a seven-dollar merlot tastes more like merlot is *meant* to than some 40-dollar merlots do? In fact, if there's any criticism of this wine it is that it's too merlot-y. Like one of those nice, soft, naive people who are just so nice that they end up getting exploited and trodden on all the time and it's really frustrating. The key to this wine is to treat it with a warm spirit and a generous mind. Its gentle, sweet, and instantly plummy flavours might be a bit of a candle in the wind (or even a yellow brick road) but enjoy them while they're there – and for what they are.

INCIDENTALS We said above that this wine lacks a bit of backbone. However, unlike those frustrating people with no backbone we compared it to, you can actually fix this merlot, and not with therapy either. Simply mix two-thirds of it with a third of a bolshie red or the Moondah Brook Merlot on page 23. Hey presto, you've got merlot with backbone.

YALUMBA Merlot 2002
$10

Here's a merlot that takes you back to your childhood when your aunty was cooking satsuma plum jam on the stove, while your uncle was mowing the kikuyu lawn outside. It's a strange blend of both aromas. This certainly isn't girlot merlot. She plays rugby, swears like a trooper and fixes her own car. Thank goodness there are a few ballsy merlots around to counter the wuss-bag reputation this much misrepresented grape variety suffers. The Yalumba is a three-phase wine: that plum-jam aroma we talked about, a bit of juicy berry fruit and the bang – whammo tannins that tug at the cheeks and gums. The experience is strangely satisfying . . .

INCIDENTALS Merlot's ancestral home is Bordeaux in the Gironde region of south-western France from whence cabernet, its sister, also comes. Merlot being earlier ripening, a little more abundant in its crop, and slightly more plummy and fleshy to taste, is used there – and here – to counter its sister's opposite personality.

PENFOLDS Rawson's Retreat Merlot 2002
$10

As this merlot pours from the bottle, you're immediately reassured by the colour: it's not wussy and it's not brown. It's a bold garnet. The smell is a bit exotic, like walking into a Tasmanian woodcraft shop: Huon pine, lemon myrtle, blackwood and sassafras . . . And behind all this there's a distant whiff of violet and the slightest hint of aniseed. For merlot, which is supposed to be as cute as a bug's ear, it's surprisingly mouth-filling and gruff, like Australian red wine should be. But at the same time, there's merlot smoothness present, as if the edges have been planed and sanded.

INCIDENTALS We've recently written a beer guide called *Beer: Slabs, Stubbies and Six-Packs* (how's that for cross-promotional branding?) and during our tasting sessions, we noticed that a lot of big-brewing-company beers had a signature flavour or smell. For instance, at CUB it was this recurring sweet-and-sour yeast-and-hop characteristic. Penfolds is the same, but here it's added tannin . . .

FIREFLY Shiraz 2002
$9

If this wine were two dollars cheaper we'd be seriously raving about it. It certainly looks like it's about a seven-dollar wine – check the label. (It probably is $7 if you look out for it discounted.) This cheap shiraz has an appeal that stems more from personality than technology. Like a person who only irons the front panels of his shirt, leaving the back all crinkly, it comes across as fresh, pure, and well laundered; then it turns its back and it's a bit unkempt. Smells of fresh red berries, those Redskin lollies again, and juicy fruit intermingled with more stinky meaty (but nevertheless interesting) aromas. It's just gruff enough to satisfy serious red drinkers.

INCIDENTALS This wine makes the point of being night-harvested. This means not that some poor vineyard worker was out in the vineyard with a torch picking grapes in the pitch black, but that a bloke drove around the vineyard on his massive machine picker on high beam listening to Led Zeppelin CDs all night. Still it makes for fresher, better wine . . .

YALUMBA Galway Shiraz 2001
$10

Watch the price on this wine because it is often discounted – sometimes as low as $8. Anyone who has been poor for a long time will have already established a relationship with this survival ration. This version sees the wine enter its seventh decade. The 2001 is a strong workaday wine with a bit more depth, structure and flavour than you get from a lot of cheap bottled red. With hybrid raspberry–blackberry fruit flavours, a little polished floorboard, and a solid but not cranky grip, it finishes lingeringly – and longer than the price-tag would suggest.

INCIDENTALS In this wine we think we've found a good companion for cheap butchers' sausages. It's got enough acid and structure to cut through and complement the mixture of fat, sawdust, breadcrumbs, salt, and small amount of meat that we call 'snags'. We suspect the winemaker eats a lot of sausages . . .

TYRRELL'S Old Winery Shiraz 2001
$12

Old winery indeed; thank goodness this very drinkable and satisfying big mouthful of red wine has the glorious taint of things slightly aged and bucolic. The Hunter Valley was renowned for this style of winemaking and it's good to see this youngster wearing the genetic thumbprint so boldly. Smells of freshly tanned leather, dust, blackberries, mulberries and then some aggressive gruff tannins followed by the bite that comes from 13.8 per cent alcohol by volume . . . Yes, you've got a powerful survival ration. And there's a secret weapon . . .

INCIDENTALS . . . Heathcote. It might start with an 'h', but it's a fair way from the Hunter Valley. Heathcote is in central Victoria. Tyrrell's have bought land there because they – and a lot of other Australian shiraz makers – have recognised this region's shiraz potential. Tyrrell's young Heathcote vineyard gives this Old Winery cheapie a good kick in the arse.

STEPPING STONE Padthaway Shiraz 2001
$12

We raved about the first Stepping Stone product in last year's guide – a cabernet sauvignon. And while most brand extensions disappoint – BMW mountain bikes, Swatch cars, Paul Newman spaghetti sauce, Madonna the actress – this shiraz is a worthy extension. It's very definitely shiraz too, with plenty of spice, a rich fruit blend of berries and plums, and well-utilised dry yet ripe tannins. The oak is there but it's subservient to shiraz – the way it should be. There are far more expensive shirazes than this, but they are much less satisfying.

INCIDENTALS It's said that Australia has the most competitive TV industry in the world. But it doesn't compare to wine. So competitive is the Australian wine industry at and around this price – $12 – that the big wine companies virtually kill each other for 'market share'. The end result is good-value wines like this. If you find one you like, buy up big and live on it.

SURVIVAL WINES

TATACHILLA Breakneck Creek Shiraz 2002
$12

The shirt-staining colour of this wine tells you straight away this is a young'un. 'Elemental' is the wine-tosser word for such raw red wine. Elemental means you're getting pure, freshly fermented shiraz. The juicy fruit flavours and smells ring out – liquorice allsorts, red jubes, and furry blackberries. The potential to become liquid confectionery is saved by a whack of South Australian tannin. It's an honest debutant for Tatachilla – and good value, particularly if you're looking for plenty of flavour. You'll get it here, by the spadeful.

INCIDENTALS And one other really good thing about this wine is that because it's cheapish the winemaker hasn't been able to paralyse the fruit flavours with expensive oak resin. The 'no wood, no good' days are thankfully in decline. Too much oak is a joke, no wood is better. The wine is more compatible with food, for a start . . .

LEASINGHAM Bastion Clare Valley Shiraz Cabernet Sauvignon 2001
$14

When cab drivers learn what we do for a living they invariably ask the same question: 'What's a good, cheap red, mate?' Invariably we reply with the same answer: 'Leasingham Bastion'. It's one of those wines that, no matter which way you look at it, represents tremendous value – even to cab drivers. It has that addictive dustiness that somehow finds its way into Clare shiraz, and the cabernet sauvignon gives it a good long satisfying grip that even satisfies Vladimir, the vodka-drinking, chain-smoking Russian taxi driver we always seem to get. No matter what city we're in.

INCIDENTALS We did a little survey of the range of prices being asked for Bastion. We found it to be as low as $10 and as high as $15. At one large retailer, if you bought a dozen, you could even get it for $9! The message is simple. Take $108 (and no more) and go and get a case. With a bit of luck it'll last you a week . . .

SEAVIEW Sparkling Shiraz
$9

This is poor man's piss-up grog. And, in a way, that's exactly fizzy red wine's purpose. You've got everything in one package: all the excitement of the popping cork, the ejaculatory effect of sparkling wine, the bubbles taking the 13.5 per cent alcohol into your blood stream very quickly, the celebratory mood created by fizz, and the joy that is given to all and sundry by shiraz . . . Squished gentle mulberry smells and aromas of mushrooms in paper bags; tastes of blackberry syrup and tinned blackberry jam; and a fair bit of party-hard sweetness. The finish is just hard enough. Serve near-frozen.

INCIDENTALS When you open bottles of sparkling wine be sure to keep the bottle on a slight angle as you rotate the cork out of the neck – and keep a thumb over the top of the cork too, or it will become a bullet and, subsequently, the wine inside will become a stain on the carpet . . .

PENFOLDS Club Reserve Aged Tawny
$13

This port offers amazing luxury to the impoverished wine addict. Perfectly suited for a quiet night with a bit of budget Danish blue or, if you don't have enough money for that, the last cigar you pinched from your uncle's wedding – he's onto his third marriage and the cigars are so good you're hoping for a fourth . . . Rich butter and nuts just on the turn; an attractively heady, spirituous, volatile aroma; and a little bit of shellacked furniture ushers in a mouthful of rich complexity that reminds us of a brandy-soaked Christmas cake. The spirit divides and conquers the tawny's potentially sickly and cloying girth, making it highly drinkable.

INCIDENTALS Why is the Club Reserve Aged Tawny so cheap? Because there's no one in the club any more. The silly old duffers are either all dead or on a drip in the nursing home. An older generation of Australians drank port; the new breed of café latte kids prefer shit like Limoncello . . . what a wasted opportunity. This forgotten wine – well, its price says it all . . .

CHAPTER THREE
ESTABLISHMENT WINES

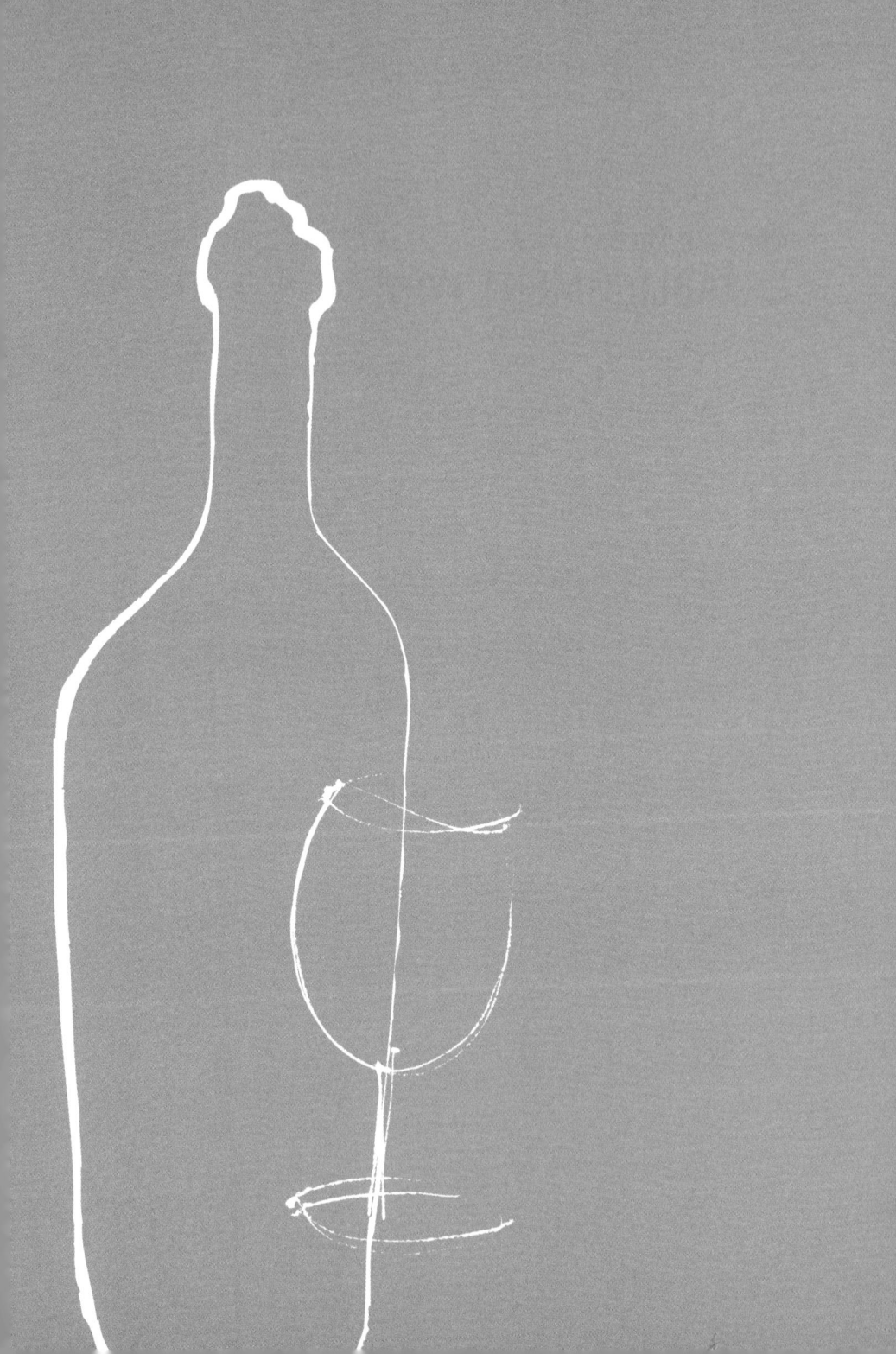

Chapter Three
ESTABLISHMENT WINES

Mandy has an uncle, Uncle Miles. He's an insurance fund manager. He knows a lot about wine. Mandy and Rohan know that because he constantly tells them. Apparently he purchased his 7 Series BMW with the returns on prudent wine investment: 'Rohan and, er, Mandy, in my experience with wine *now* is the time to invest in some – what I like to call – blue-chip premium reds; Rohan, such wines – I can easily provide you with a list if you'd like – have, since '93, outstripped blue-chip share returns by a factor of 223 per cent – and that is a very conservative figure, Rohan, let me assure you . . .'

They have to go around to Uncle Miles's place for dinner. Miles's wife, Jeannie, serves crayfish tails – one each . . . Then they get a mini boeuf tournado for the main course. Rohan had been quite excited about all of this – he thought they'd get some pretty poncy wine with dinner. Ro had even lashed out and taken a bottle of champagne – Lanson Black Label. Everyone loved this, although Miles graciously admitted he preferred Dom – 'I have some excellent back vintages in one of the Eurocaves.' The Eurocave? Rohan's photographic memory dredged out an image of one of those things from a wine-magazine ad. A Eurocave is a big climate-controlled fridge sort of thing for storing – sorry, cellaring – wine. They hold 200 bottles and cost $8000, empty . . .

With the lobster tails Rohan had expected possibly a fine chablis, or even a Pouilly-Fusse, or a Montrachet, or some other 'serious' white burgundy he'd read about but never tasted. What they got was a 13-year-old Roxburgh Chardonnay. Miles made a big fuss over this wine. It was the colour of Phar Lap's urine – after the big race . . . It tasted like a mixture of old tinned pineapple juice, retsina and sherry. Mandy had to kick Rohan under the table a couple of times, such was the revolting effect this aged white product had on his facial muscles. But Mandy had already decided the best approach to dealing with Miles was to get as drunk as possible, and as quickly as possible. At least she had Jeannie for company in this endeavour . . .

A cheap Riverland red accompanied the beef. Rohan recognised it and knew it cost about $10. That's when the penny dropped. Miles was a *wine investor*, not a wine drinker. He liked the cachet that wine – and 'fine wine' and its associated lore – brought, but he didn't really like drinking it. Rohan reckoned that Miles probably didn't even have any personal, empirical wine knowledge. Miles knew about wine books and wine magazines and the secondary wine auction market and how much a bottle of Black Stump Double Oaked Shiraz was worth at five years of age, but that was where it stopped. Miles was on the dark side. He'd forgotten that wine was a drink. To him, it had all the flavour, texture, appeal, and gustatory comfort of a stock prospectus.

Driving home after dinner Rohan didn't have to worry about RBTs or booze buses: he'd hardly drunk anything. Mandy was strangely silent; she felt uncomfortable – full of too much crayfish and much too much awful chardonnay. Just as they were turning into Boulting Crescent, Mandy turned to Rohan and slurred, 'If you ever turn out like Uncle Milezzz, Rohan, you're dropped. Now take me inzzzide, darling . . .'

PIPERS BROOK Reserve Chardonnay 2000
$45

establishment winner

Here is an Australian chardonnay that is handling its three-year age with quite a bit of grace. There's richness and honeyed nuttiness that come from those few years of bottle age, but these cool-climate Tasmanian chardonnay grapes have enough natural acid inside them to counter the unctuousness. The acid encases the wine in a crystal clear and intensely clean sheen of mouth puckering, minerally, mouth-salivating tautness. This is the sort of wine you should buy on your birthday and drink over a particularly long lunch – by yourself.

INCIDENTALS Three years is old for an Australian chardonnay. If one year for a dog equals seven human years, one year for an Australian chardonnay equals about 35 . . . That means that five-year-old chardonnays are well and truly dead; this grand old man is looking very good indeed, even though he received his telegram from the Queen five years ago . . .

ESTABLISHMENT WINES

PIRIE 1998
$55

Pirie is a bubbly that gets a big tick on all the things that make for good fizz. The colour has that ambiguous clear, glowing lemon gold – it's awfully inviting. The bubbles rise to the top of the glass as if computer controlled, and gather together in a ring of mousse of just the right thickness around the inside of the glass. It has that smell of slightly bitter almond-meal biscuits with a hint of Bonox – the result of careful yeast use. Its most striking feature is clean power – a polished silver bullet of complex flavours that leaves no wound . . .

INCIDENTALS The man for whom this wine is named, or perhaps, the wine for whom this man was named, Andrew Pirie, no longer works for the winery he established. He forms an elite club of winemakers whose name remains the property of someone else: Andrew Garrett, Tim Knappstein, Wolf Blass and the Hardys. We wonder at the psychological effect of this. Do they feel as if a small part of them is lying lost out in a vineyard somewhere?

BOLLINGER Champagne Special Cuvée
$80-ish

One of the characteristics of great champagne is that when it goes flat you still like drinking it – the 'base' wine is still the real deal. Flat Bollinger is a fine beverage in its own right – a perfect match for crayfish, in fact. One sniff tells you of the care gone into the preparation: almond meal and brioche – but much better than any almond or bread you've ever smelled. Fruity aromas reside in here, too, but they are an amalgam of lots of things: from off apples to strawberries, orange skins, stone fruits, citrus . . . Add the bubble to all of this and the flavours are turbo charged. Oh, and we think Bollinger is a little softer, or 'new age', than it used to be . . .

INCIDENTALS Masculine or feminine? Is your champagne a boy or a girl? This is an ever-popular game to play when you are getting blind on this French fizzy *produit*. Masculine styles are firm, acidic, require food, are low on fluff factor and big on power. They are more one-glass champagnes than the whole bottle. Feminine styles are creamier, seem sweeter by being less harshly acidic, yet can still carry some punch. Bollinger *est un homme*.

LEASINGHAM Bin 7 Clare Valley Riesling 2002
$16

Like Australia's great motoring icons – the Commodore and the Falcon – Bin 7 has a long history, and a long history of model changes. It's been rounded, it's been rough, it's been supercharged, and discounted; it's been almost dismissed, but it has always managed to hang on. The 2002 model, if it were an automobile, would probably be car of the year. Star-bright with a pale gold duco, there's honeysuckle, citrus blossom and something that reminds us of that lemon juice, water and honey drink that you got when you were a sore-throated kid. And the lemons were those slightly under-ripe ones, although there's nothing under-ripe about this wine.

INCIDENTALS It's not only the tradition that makes this riesling establishment, it's the fact that, unlike a lot of establishment pretenders, this is a wine that will actually repay cellaring – which is something we've noticed that all those upper-crusty types seem to want to do with wine. If you do cellar this wine, you'll lose a bit of the freshness and get a bit of toasty honey coming to the fore. It's your choice.

JACOB'S CREEK Reserve Riesling 2001
$15

Rocking up to a quality dinner party with a bottle of Jacob's Creek Riesling in tow may get some of the snobs sneering, but this is Jacob's Creek *Reserve* Riesling, darling – same genus, different species. Its aroma is hyper-classic Australian riesling, too: limes, river pebbles and a whiff of petroleum. It has intensity in your mouth; indeed, it's more like white wine than fleeting, ethereal riesling. It can also handle strongly flavoured fish. So when they serve the sautéed scallops, your bottle of Jacob's Creek Reserve will provide both the richness and minerality to simultaneously complement and counter the little molluscs.

INCIDENTALS Jacob's Creek? Establishment? Yes, after all, Jacob's Creek is Australia's greatest wine diplomat. Jacob's Creek has even won Australia's greatest wine honour – the Maurice O'Shea award. All around the world its name is synonymous with affordable, good-quality Australian wine. The name itself is somewhat ironic: in volume terms the brand is less of a little creek and more of a vast ocean.

STARVEDOG LANE Sauvignon Blanc 2002
$19

Not your standard sauvignon blanc, this fancy 19-dollar product whispers rather than shouts its aromas and flavours: nettles, nectarines, guava, gooseberry, grapes such as Waltham Cross, and Singer sewing-machine oil. That's a fair bit, but it goes further. Once past the teeth, there's an impression of incredible richness – all commanding and out of focus. But just as you're registering that, salty acid pulls the whole thing into really sharp extra-close-up and once more you're concentrating on the aforementioned minutiae. It's a documentary . . .

INCIDENTALS Why are all decent sauvignon blancs $19? We believe that there is a very sinister reason – price collusion. Yes, we hate to be the bearers of such news, but we have taped conversations, stolen faxed documents and sworn eye-witness accounts that the price of decent sauvignon blanc is fixed by large wine companies. This year it's $19.

MCWILLIAMS Elizabeth Semillon 1999
$16

Quite golden and pale – a little like Her Majesty in a way – this semillon is about as cleansing as white wine can get. Attractively acidic, with that lemon-and-honey tang you get in throat soothers, there are some wonderful secondary flavours already appearing: vanilla, wet stones, fresh rain . . . Whether you drink it now, with those traces of lychees in the aroma and taste, or let it stay in the cellar for another five years, whence it will produce more toasty and polished-floorboard effects, is entirely up to your own taste. Whatever you do, buy at least two bottles – and it's only 11 per cent alcohol.

INCIDENTALS Like the monarchy, this wine represents an anachronistic institution. No, we don't mean McWilliams. We mean the way that this wine receives some bottle ageing at the winery before it's released. No one does this any more – it just costs too much money. Most winemakers want the stuff to be made, bottled and flogged off pronto. Thank goodness McWs are hanging on to the tradition.

ROSEMOUNT Show Reserve Semillon 2002
$23

The smell of this semillon provides an immediate mental picture. Poncy suburb; moderately warm day; north-facing sunroom; expensive Danish designer, steam-bent, lacquered white furniture . . . The mistress of the house – in broad-brimmed hat – is pruning the lemon trees outside. Her effeminate husband – in neatly pressed cream linen pants – is placing freshly cut gardenias in a very expensive vase. He's sucking a Fantale lolly and there's some Vivaldi playing in the background; he's thinking about preparing a fusion salad for lunch . . .

INCIDENTALS Semillon. Or semillon and oak. Semillon made in a stainless-steel tank is all grass, citrus and acid; indeed, so mean and lean is this type of wine that some people refer to it as acidulated water or even battery acid.
To counter this, some winemakers ferment or mature a percentage of their semillon in oak barrels – the oak adding richness, roundness and resinousness countering the harsh acidity.

JACOB'S CREEK Limited Release Chardonnay 2001
$24

Just from the look of this wine you can tell that it means business. This is no standard Jacob's Creek chardy. It's got a star-bright colour and a fair degree of viscosity. There's not a single whiff of pineapple, butterscotch or vanilla in its smell; instead there's custard fruit, marzipan and solvents. The texture is slick and speedy, and the thing that really makes this wine – its structure – is strong boned. This is not another cartilaginous chardonnay. And we love the way it signs off. It's a self-cleaning chardonnay finishing with a mineral-water-like rinse.

INCIDENTALS Jacob's Creek is three-tiered nowadays: the standard cheapie, the reserve, and this limited-release example. You can tell this is the most important pony in the paddock because each bottle has its own number. Our one was 20325 . . . One wonders what the point is. Once you've drunk 20325 you can hardly look for it again – or are you meant to collect the whole set?

HOWARD PARK Western Australia Chardonnay 2001
$35

This chardonnay is very instructive. For a start, it helps you to understand why grapefruit is called grapefruit. This is the key flavour in this wine, but there are many other citrus fruits here as well: old oranges, kumquats, slightly green lemons and West Indian limes. But it's not just vitamin C. There's some spicy oak notes, fresh coconut flesh (try saying that when you're pissed) and, well, more vitamin C . . . It's a taut, steely, fresh and decongesting chardonnay. It would make a very healthy breakfast.

INCIDENTALS Before chardonnays like this one, the reason grapefruit was called grapefruit remained one of the world's unsolved mysteries. Grapefruit doesn't taste like a grape and certainly doesn't look like one. But when chardonnay grapes are grown lean and mean in cooler climates and made into wine, *voila*, fermented grapefruit juice. Isn't nature wonderful?

SHAW AND SMITH M3 Vineyard Chardonnay 2001
$34

Lemony viscosity and a lace of posh oak-barrel spice fly up your nose as soon as the glass comes into olfactory range. Intense mineral salts dominate your mouth. The acidity is at the grapefruit end of the bucket – but it's quality stuff. Here's a taut and lean – even spare – chardonnay that really gets poncy chardy drinkers excited. Maybe, just maybe, the wacky winemakers have picked and made this vintage of chardy a little more tightly wound than previous years. They're looking for a chardonnay that will actually age and change – possibly for the better – in the bottle.

INCIDENTALS One of this wine's winemakers went to see the Rolling Stones the last time the band was in Australia. Which leads one to wonder (if you've got nothing better to do) if chardonnay styles were Rolling Stones' songs, which song would the M3 be? It's certainly no 'Brown Sugar' or melodramatic 'Angie'; it's more contained, more like 'Wild Horses' – at least musically . . .

WIRRA WIRRA Adelaide Hills Chardonnay 2002
$25

Greg's fridge (it's more like a biosphere) held three chardies. The first two (another Adelaide Hills posh product and a Hunter Valley thing) were a waste of refrigeration. We thought that a McLaren Vale winemaker might not be capable of wending their way through the twists and turns of cool-climate Adelaide Hills chardy. We were wrong. They could. They had. Pool salts, oyster shells, cashews, a trace of tinned fruit, and some classy oak-cum-camphor aromas. It's more aggressive to smell than to taste; but it's gentle on the tastebuds and drinkable to boot – so we drank it . . .

INCIDENTALS The Adelaide Hills are a posh place to live – whether you're a person or a grape. Even the wheelie bins up there carry themselves with a certain air. Alexander Downer lives up there. The people of the Adelaide Hills refer to themselves as 'us' – and others as 'them' . . . No wonder the grapes have a crisp, reserved, restrained cool style.

YERING STATION Chardonnay 2001
$20

Poncy dinner parties and fine-wine events can become very, very boring – all small talk and being polite. That's when this establishment chardonnay can come into its own. This is a wine that will polarise people like never before. It has some really strange aromas. One reminded us of the 'B' part of Araldite; there's also some pretty full-on deli produce (pastrami), and even some weird body aroma – the scent of a woman? The taste is salty and savoury, which makes it a great condiment for so many foods.

INCIDENTALS Style is an odd concept when it comes to ocker chardy. The great majority of it is rich, alcoholic, gushy, tropical-fruit lolly water. Some winemakers, however, want to swim against this sickly tide. They want to make a wine outside the norm; and while it might not have such widespread popular appeal, to its fans it's the most drinkable chardonnay around.

TYRRELL'S Vat 47 Chardonnay 2001
$45

Like a well-spoken sentence (we don't know very much about those), this wine is all about structure. It's not a textbook lesson in chardonnay grammar – thankfully it's got its own style. There's some classic ocker chardonnay aromas up front – buttered nuts, ripe quinces . . . But then there's some weird shit going on: pool chlorine, salt licks, and the juice of a seriously under-ripe lemon. The finish pulls all these disparate parts together. They say the finish maketh the wine – this one really lingers with the distant hint of lemony oak. Such a finish makes its own demands . . .

INCIDENTALS . . . and those demands concern food. Any hard oak resin flavours in chardonnay can destroy its ability to be an unaccompanied drink. This one – with all its structure – wants a roast chook with some garlic and herbs shoved up its cloaca. After you've roasted it let the bird rest breast-side down for 10 minutes before you tear it to bits. Serve with said chardonnay.

PIPERS BROOK Estate Pinot Noir 2002
$36

Riddled with establishmentarianism (from price to label to taste), this wine nevertheless pulls some strange moves: decaying bodies of European sports cars in a humus-rich paddock. In this sports car there's also a woman's handbag where all of those aromas of old lanolin-based lipsticks, bits of fossilising chocolate, and faded, perfumed handkerchiefs have mixed with the fine yet similarly decaying leather of the Italian bag. The humus-rich soil does wonderful things for the old cherry trees and the wild strawberries growing all around the car. Posh, complex, structured.

INCIDENTALS What can pinot cure? Well, it doesn't really fix hunger or alcoholic thirst, but it can work well on the world-weary, the excessively contemplative, or a little blue mood. It can also match your thought process and give back as much to you as you give to it. Then it becomes a real and trustworthy friend.

DE BORTOLI Yarra Valley Pinot Noir 2000
$29

In many ways $29 is quite a good price for this wine, particularly given it could be your last chance to taste the merits of the 2000 vintage in the Yarra. It was a strange year up there – the sun shined and it didn't rain every day. In this stylish, taut, elegant and – in many ways – faux burgundy, you get aromas of air-dried and preserved meats in a pinus radiata forest. It's a picnic. Someone's brought along a rhubarb pie and a bottle of preserved sour cherries to finish things off.

INCIDENTALS This wine will absolutely come into its own if you fix a meal to suit its needs. It's not that it's needy; it's just lean and stern, requiring a little fat and something a little gamy. We suggest some duck confit, rabbit-and-pork terrine, field-mushroom-and-chicken-stock risotto, and the like.

BROWN BROTHERS Shiraz 2001
$19

Even urban Australians can't help liking the smell of eucalypt. From the moment the leaves, twigs or branches go on the barbie or into the fire, there is something that speaks to us all. Is it your inner child remembering holidays? If that is the case, this is a liquid version of that same experience. From the region around Milawa in the north-east of Victoria (near the snowfields) this wine exhibits eucalyptus; sweet, ripe mulberry fruit; and a touch of creosote. Mushroom compost mix, earth, and a pleasantly tart finish help keep the package taut and restrained. This is classy wine worthy of classy people. Good value, too.

INCIDENTALS At Brown Brothers' cellar door – one of the most popular and celebrated in the region – they have about a million wines available to taste. Actually, the number is 54, but when you've been in a bus since 8 am and it's the third day of the footy trip, it seems like a million. Tips? Don't be afraid to spit wine out when you're tasting . . .

REDMAN Coonawarra Shiraz 2001
$17

Aniseed and fennel, ouzo, Pernod, Pastis . . . These are the smells this cool-climate shiraz leads with. It is definitely herbal before it is anything else. Berry flavours eventually emerge, but they're sour loganberries. The emphasis here is on structure rather than flesh, and this makes for a long, cool, clean wine – a red that purifies. Faint nut skins come to the fore as the wine signs off; the texture and tannins linger with grace. It is a red that cuts through the bullshit.

INCIDENTALS We bag cellaring a fair bit, you may have noticed. The Redman is a wine that has the structure and composition to make us think that three to five years downstairs in the wine-bunker mightn't be a bad thing. It will not flab out or go all oak-sick. The bones are there to handle the weight that age brings.

CAPE MENTELLE Shiraz 2001
$28

This might be an establishment shiraz but its nose is a bit feral – like a kombi full of greenies on a trip to save the Karri Forest in WA: rotting kangaroos on the side of the road, whiffs of the Australian bush, BLT sangers, homemade blackberry jam on toast . . . One greenie is new to the game and he's got a pair of brand-new Blundstones on. The kombi's door seals have perished and there's a bit of dust coming in; the travellers can all taste it in their mouths – dry and earthy. After only one day the vegos are being strangely affected by the bacon sangers; they're dreaming of roasted meats – beef, lamb, pork . . .

INCIDENTALS This is a funky wine without a doubt, but it has establishment credentials: its name, Cape Mentelle; its region, Margaret River; the fact that it's owned by a poncy French champagne house and that it's just expensive enough for you to be taken seriously . . .

MOUNT LANGI GHIRAN Cliff Edge Shiraz 2001
$28

If the first thing that makes you excited about this wine are the three words 'Mount Langi Ghiran' you are probably a wine tosser. And you need help. Langi's shiraz has a ridiculous reputation and a high price-tag. This Cliff Edge product comes from a cliff-edge site at Mount LG, in western Victoria. It smells of every type of pepper you've ever known, from quality black to cafeteria white. There's also a lovely whiff of the Australian bush, and some of those savoury, smoked-meat smells that come from devilish, if unsubtle, oak-barrel work. But check the acidity and the grip once the wine is inside your mouth!

INCIDENTALS This wine is half the price of the poncy Langi shiraz the wine tossers go gooey over. Its interest lies with the more hard-core pepper and spice flavours that typify so well shiraz grown in cold areas. This could be a really good present for one of your wine friends who's been living overseas for a while and is craving stylish Aussie reds.

YERING STATION Reserve Shiraz 2001
$55

The first thing that we love about this wine is the fantastic smell, all derived from clever oak-barrel use and shiraz grown in the cool Yarra Valley: pepper, smoked bacon, cap guns, charcuterie . . . It's an enticing smell that softens up your cynical mind for the sour plum flavours that follow. It is dry yet plush, too; the dryness coming from shiraz skins, the plushness from the concentrated juice of those same grapes' flesh.

INCIDENTALS Ben once used a computer simulator to make Yarra Valley Shiraz. It was on an interactive touch screen in Adelaide's Australian Wine Centre. He did everything to his Yarra Valley shiraz that Yering Station have done to this wine. At the end of the simulation the computer gives you a score; it gave Ben 14 out of 20. It suggested that the problem lay in the fruit's regional source . . .

MITCHELTON Central Victoria Shiraz 2001
$21

Central Victoria is a dry part of that strange state that enjoys (at least as far as vines go) pretty tough soil and cool nights – or as the wine tossers say, 'a big diurnal effect'. Along with the fact that this wine is made from shiraz grapes, this helps to explain the smells and flavours herein: eucalyptus, clay, ironbark, green peppercorn, tree sap and – perhaps this wine's most discernible feature – a huge tannic wallop. At this stage in its life it's as gruff as buggery, but if you're into that form of self-administered discipline otherwise known as wine cellaring, it's just the ticket.

INCIDENTALS When you're stumped for a gift to present to one of your silly old ginned-up buffer mates, we've got a tip. Such people seem to like nothing better than wines such as this. They equate drinkability with pain. This wine needs a year or two to smooth out, or try decanting it and serving with fatty meats. Or give it to the silly old buffer . . .

GRANT BURGE The Holy Trinity Grenache Shiraz Mourvèdre
$33

This is a two-edged wine. While on the one hand it has heaps of power, on the other it's quite delicate and refined. Winemakers try to create this sort of alchemy all the time and it's really quite difficult. Good fruit and fancy-pants oak help, and the Holy Trinity has plenty of that. Like a heavily built bloke whose real tastes might lie with beer, this wine has been well educated, observes a careful low-fat diet, and is in pretty good shape. More tall than wide, at the moment he passes the pinch test. But there is some paunch lurking in the middle – he's careful to keep his gut tucked in as well.

INCIDENTALS Why are we recommending this as an establishment wine? It's the combination of power and refinement. Whoever you serve this to will know they're getting some serious red wine, but it won't knock them around so much as to make them wish – come the next morning – they'd not met you.

GRANT BURGE Cameron Vale Cabernet Sauvignon 2001
$24

For a few years now Grant Burge red wines, while they've been popular, have had a bit of a reputation for being 'oak-fucked'. This is a technical term meaning the wine has too much oak flavour . . . But things have changed at Maison Burge; a couple of trips to France and the style is back on the rails. This slick cabernet is rich blackberry and cassis and antique shops in provincial France. The smell suggests a dry texture. Dry it is, but once inside your mouth the wine is nicely tight and even a little bit berry sour. These qualities make it a fantastic red for Scotch fillet.

INCIDENTALS Grant Burge hit the Australian wine scene with a bloke called Wilson in the late 1970s and made wines at Krondorf. They blew people away. He sold Krondorf in very much a Kerry Packer/Alan Bond/Channel Nine sort of situation, and being a proud Barossa Valerinarean, has spent the money buying sizable chunks of the Barossa's best vineyards. He now drives a Porsche and wears leather pants.

RYMILL Cabernet Sauvignon 1999
$28

Cab sav is one of life's frustrating grape varieties. Blessed with much more colour and tannin than most of its red relations it can be a very incomplete experience. Like fish without chips, or curry without rice, you can feel that something is missing. That's definitely not the case here. This bottle-aged Coonawarra-grown product with the stallions kicking the shit out of each other on the label – a metaphor for Coonawarra's dirty local politics – is a very complete wine indeed. From start to finish there's a procession of subtle flavours and textures that fit together without you noticing the joins. It's what the establishment call 'an integrated wine'.

INCIDENTALS Integration is a classic wine-tosser word, but one that for once actually means something. The *Oxford English Dictionary* cites it as a 'thing complete in itself' and, with wine, it means you can't pick out where grapes, oak and winemaker's aftershave start and finish.

MILDARA Coonawarra Cabernet Sauvignon 2000
$30

This is honest Australian cabernet. It used to be a favourite of honest Australians who cellared wine. But, as we all know, they're a dying breed. Mildara Coonawarra cab sav surprisingly lives on. It comes from a company that rarely allows such 'challenging' wines out on to the street. But more power to the right arm of whoever made (or didn't make) the decision. It's bay leaf, dark chocolate, blackberry nip, and a hint of sage leaf; once inside your mouth it's a big, rich, tannin-studded, teeth-staining monster. Which would suggest . . .

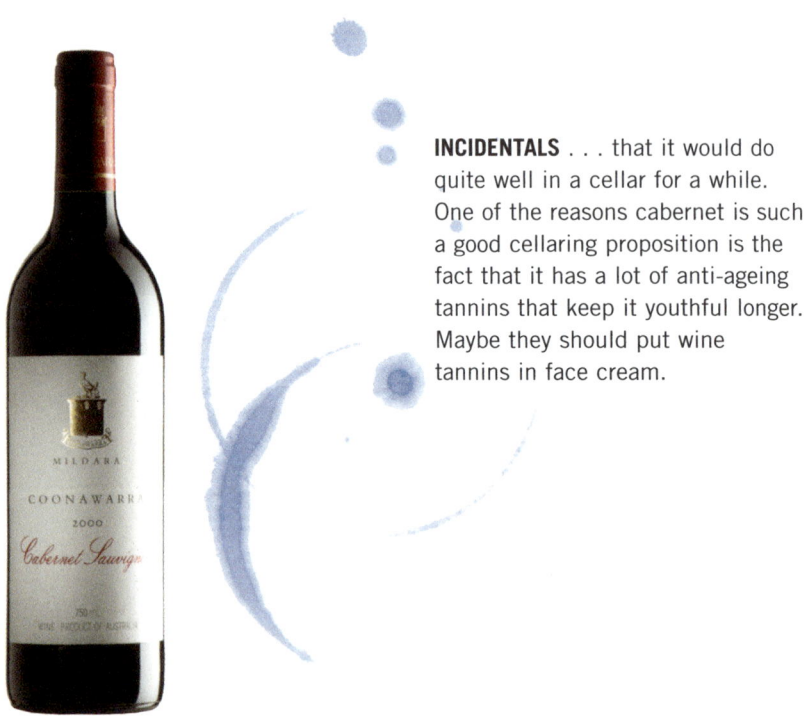

INCIDENTALS . . . that it would do quite well in a cellar for a while. One of the reasons cabernet is such a good cellaring proposition is the fact that it has a lot of anti-ageing tannins that keep it youthful longer. Maybe they should put wine tannins in face cream.

MITCHELTON Blackwood Park Botrytis Riesling 2002
$17 (375 ml)

Botrytis means sweet and sticky. Fortunately, this sweet and sticky riesling is not overblown with those qualities – as many botrytised wines tend to be. Acidity still needs to be present to balance the wine. Paler in colour than its glueier, tackier half-bottled mates, this Mitchelton still retains the smells of lime and lemon – those riesling aromas; but it's got sweet honeysuckle and lime cordy, too. Imagine making lime marmalade and you've got the taste. The acidity rides in halfway through, and saves you from that revolting, cloying mouth massacre typical of the brethren . . .

INCIDENTALS Botrytis can be likened to those aliens in sci-fi films who take over a human host and transform him or her into a green, oozing and generally unattractive blob. In this case the grape is the host and the fungus is the alien. Too much botrytis (the alien) and the flavours of the resultant wine bear no relation to the original host. If there's just enough botrytis you get a wine like this one. Balanced.

CHAPTER FOUR
SENSUAL WINES

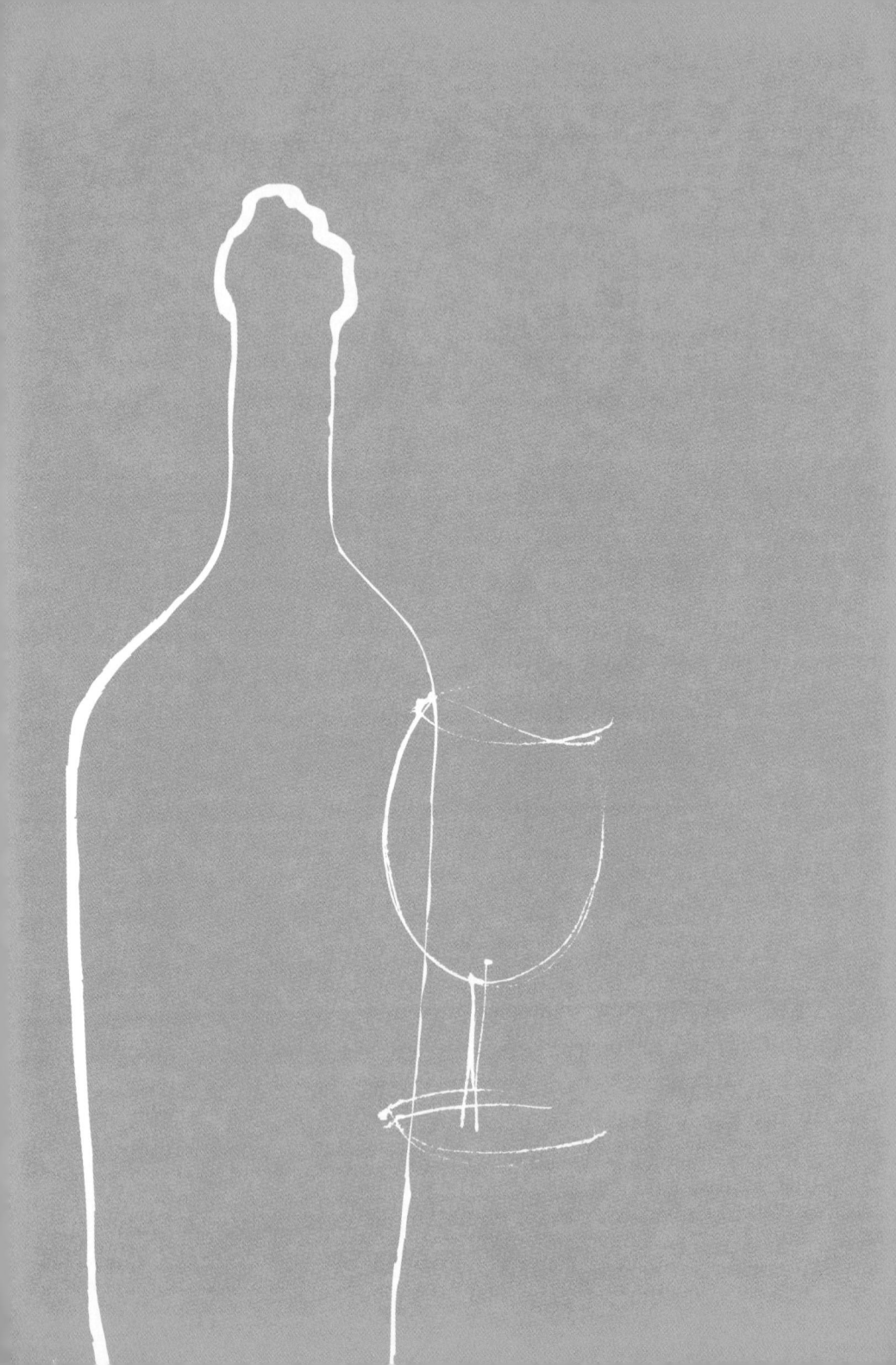

Chapter Four
SENSUAL WINES

Mandy and Rohan haven't had sex for eight whole days. It's not anyone's fault, it's just not happening. But why?

Rohan finally got that job he was after and it's goodbye to the lubricated ultrasound module and the portable imaging machine. No more looking at footballers' anterior interior excruciate ligaments or pregnant women's placentae. He's now managing the imaging department of a boutique private hospital. The food's even good, and they serve wine with meals – at least to the patients. But Rohan, well, he's not drinking much, and his mind seems to be on other things; he hasn't lost that loving feeling, but . . .

The bedroom. Mandy is an Aquarian with her moon in Scorpio. Need we say more? She's quite driven. A lack of bedroom action makes her cranky – even gnarly. But at least she knows why she's been so short-tempered and huffy. So she spends her days at *Celebrity Now* magazine wondering how to bring Rohan's libido back from Limpido del Mar.

She plans the ultimate seduction dinner. She's conned Ro into knocking off at six, and she's chucked a sickie. It's not wrong, she justifies to herself, because she actually is sick – or she will be soon if matters don't improve . . .

Rohan is a control freak, and the trick to this dinner, she's decided, is to put him well outside the boundaries of his comfort zone. Food and wine that she knows he likes is not the answer. His star sign is Aries, and to serve him something he cooks himself means he will think he could have done it better. That's just him. But Mandy is very clever, not to mention smart; she has a woman's instincts coupled with an Aquarian's confidence.

She realises that with their budgeting of late, it's been a long time since Rohan had any really decent grog – or anything else. Mandy, with her mathematical mind, knows that a judiciously chosen wine has far more aphrodisiacal power than any food, so she decides to go for a 5:1 ratio – the wine will be allocated a budget five times that of the dinner. Rohan likes fish but doesn't tend to cook a lot of Asian food, so Mandy makes tiny Thai fishcakes from really fresh bream and serves them with a 50-dollar champagne. It's Devaux; $30 cheaper than Rohan's favourite Bollinger, but the nice bloke at Rohan's favourite poncy wine shop tells her that while it may not be as masculine as Bollinger, it is nevertheless very high quality – and drinkable. 'And I don't mean sweet,' he adds. For main course she initially plans to do salmon fillets wrapped in prosciutto cooked on the barbecue, but then she remembers how much Ro enjoys railing against 'crap hormone-infused farmed salmon', so she goes for ocean trout instead. If he gets cranky, well, she can send him out to the balcony barbecue to cool off for a while . . . Lentils and spinach will join the fish but everything will be subservient to the Tarrawarra Pinot Noir. This is the potion that will do the job on Ro. Expensive, silky, long pinot when he's least expecting it. What a weapon!

Ro arrives home full of petty complaints and still thinking very much above the belt. Someone had that very morning taken his 'clearly marked and designated parking spot'. He actually got a spot closer to his office door, but that wasn't the point, 'was it?' Furthermore, the drug-company junket to Palazzo Versace on the Gold Coast has been cancelled . . .

Ro has said all this without that really frustrated edge to his voice, and he hasn't even noticed the Devaux yet. Mandy gave him the glass as he walked in and all he's done is drink it. The Devaux has noticed him though, and the bubbles of fine French alcohol are slowly removing the patina of the day's quasi-dilemmas and beginning to reveal the real Ro.

He's off on another tirade about the number of staff smoking breaks but stops mid-sentence, looks at his glass, looks at Mandy, and notices her;

indeed, he is struck by her. She hands him a tiny Thai fishcake. It all comes back to him. She had ordered fish cakes that Tuesday night long ago at the Thai takeaway.

Half the ocean trout is eaten and Rohan and Mandy finish the pinot in a room that wasn't designed for dining.

PIZZINI Sangiovese 2002
$23

This is a lush sangiovese, as suave and sensual as the most handsome Italian–Australian soccer player. Aquiline features and a hairstyle that never needs any product, it's Michelangelo statuesque. Except his donger is a bit bigger than the standard Michelangelo issue. There's flesh on his bones – all muscle-toned and very grabbable. Or edible. Or drinkable. Whatever your preference. The smell is of where he's been: mucking around in an old cherry orchard on a hot, dusty, autumnal day. He walked back to your house via a damp forest where he gathered some mushrooms.

sensual winner

INCIDENTALS Lush, as we said, because 2002 was quite a good year in the King Valley. Being a cool region in an otherwise warm climatic zone, you – or rather the grapes – get the best of both worlds: acid and ripeness. Acid = cool weather and ripeness = sunshine. *Perfetto*. And this makes for a sangiovese (the red grape of Chianti) that's not too heady; but it is muscly, as abovementioned.

DEVAUX Grand Reserve Champagne
$53

Champagne, when it's the real deal, is always a sensual wine product, but some are more sensual than others. This is a case in point. Indeed, this bubbly is no product, it's an aphrodisiac. It's got such lovely cute, you beaut, soft little bubbles – a pretty delicacy that suggests ease and complete agreement. It's a fizz that flirts with you, suggesting different flavours at different times: a hint of peanut brittle, a bit of toasted nuts and honey, beeswaxed antique furniture, and an apple dessert. But while she flirts, there's also an assertive side. She really is quite lovely.

INCIDENTALS And just so you won't go too far, this fizz comes with its own chaperone. Check the label; she's there just above the Devaux name. Actually she's the widow Devaux. Every champagne house needs a widow or, in French, a *veuve*. Bollinger has one, Veuve Clicquot has one, Devaux has one . . . In Champagne, perfectly healthy husbands often die unexpectedly. But it's all for a good cause – marketing.

LEO BURING Clare Valley Riesling 2002
$16

We were really surprised about the price of this wine. But that's riesling. It mostly offers the best bang-to-buck ratio of all the white varieties. This is a sleek riesling – slippery sleek. The acidity is there, but it's soft. It's like someone is gently stroking you with their hand – a hand that has just been washed using a fine soap perfumed with apple-lime blossom and the faintest bit of spearmint. The aftertaste is the winner here; just when you think it's all over, this wine comes back and gives you more.

INCIDENTALS It's no coincidence that this wine is in the sensual chapter. Leo Buring, or 'Bureau' as they used to call him, was one of Australia's most legendary porn stars back in the 1950s. His films are collector's items now and very rarely seen. He was very big in Scandinavia, and in other parts . . . With his hard-earned kroner he retired to the Clare Valley and planted riesling. True story.

ORLANDO Steingarten Riesling 2001
$24

Like those people who sit quietly and don't ram their personality down your throat, Steingarten gets to know you slowly. There's confidence and obvious attraction exuding from this aromatic white; it's just that the volume is turned down. Muted smells of paspalum just catch your attention and you're drawn into conversation. Once Steingarten begins to speak, however, things really start to explode: racy flavours of apricots, minerals, and lychees zip and zing through your mouth. A casual conversation will quickly become dinner . . .

INCIDENTALS A previous vintage of this wine appeared in *Drink Drank Drunk 2002*. Back then we banged on about Steingarten being so named because of all the rocks in the vineyard – so many that they had to blast holes in the ground just to plant the vines. Ben got drunk recently with some Steingarten locals; rumour has it that the *rocks*, not the explosives, were brought in. Funny business, wine . . .

SENSUAL WINES | 113

PETER LEHMANN Reserve Semillon 1998
$24

To get right to the point, here's some sweet sweat; something bittersweet; the taste of someone's nape very early on the following morning . . . Perfume's fading and the alcohol from the seven too many glasses of wine the night before is transevaporating through the skin's pores. If you're into wine, nothing is more attractive. Her name is semillon, she's a golden blonde, and a little bit older than you think – but she can drink. She doesn't stay too long but the finish is memorable, saving her from any flippancy that she may have shown earlier on.

INCIDENTALS Some wines really do the above to you when you taste them. Sure, this five-year-old semillon has muted citrus, lemon butter and resiny astringency, but these things are not important when compared to its overall effect – its sensuous smell, taste and texture – and the memories all that evokes.

HOUGHTON Pemberton Sauvignon Blanc 2002
$22

We'll be honest from the outset. This is a wine to pick up chicks with. It will not work on men. Chicks like sauvignon blanc and this one will like them. Why? It's got the colour of an expensive French perfume; an aroma that sits – knife-edge-like – between sugar syrup and a freshly showered male body; a texture that both bites and soothes at the same time (like that fine line between pleasure and pain); and flavours of sour lychees, musk and sandalwood. Just a touch more alcohol and this could be used as an aftershave. It would work at 100 paces, through a crowded room.

INCIDENTALS Sauv blanc is good – or at least can be good – when it comes from cool regions. It needs acidity, not tropical fruit ripeness. Well, that's what we think. Pemberton is in WA – in the cooler bits down south. Like the Adelaide Hills, this region is producing some drinkable sauv blancs.

STONIER Mornington Peninsula Chardonnay 2002
$24

Girly. Creamy. These were some of the descriptors – as we call them in the wine-tossing business – that emerged from our lips while we were 'nosing' this wine. When we had finished tossing (and tasting) we decided it should go in the sensual chapter. It has an unctuousness and easy, yet stylish, good-quality confectionary appeal. Once you get past the front door and it's inside your mouth, the feng shui is pretty good. Everything is in the right place. There's nuttiness and spice; this white is toned yet curved. Best of all it's not too overt, so your attention doesn't wander from your beloved – for too long.

INCIDENTALS For the umpteenth time we find ourselves recommending the cheaper, less ponced-up stablemate in a winery's range. We don't do this on purpose; we are not pretending to be the people's palate and championing cheaper wines in order to appeal to a broader audience. It's just the way it comes out. In winemaking, as in life, more is not always better.

ISABEL Marlborough Chardonnay 2001
$29

New Zealanders make some of the best handmade chardonnay in the Southern Hemisphere. These sorts of chardonnays get truly spoiled – the vineyards are fussed over and everything is as organically grown as is economically possible. They're nursed every moment of their infant lives. And as is the case here, the results can be spectacular. Pleasantly warm and toasty, if you're more into drinking than sniffing this is a chardonnay that wins its points for its palate rather than the nose. It starts out minerally, even slightly austere, but then builds in intensity. It takes off – flying through your mouth on a winged acid structure. What a class act.

INCIDENTALS We worried that we might perhaps have a little too much chardonnay in this book, but then we realised that – with due journalistic diligence – we were only mirroring the nature of the wine market. If you hadn't noticed, there is shitloads of chardonnay out there. The ones that make it through to these pages are the best.

PEGASUS BAY Chardonnay 2001
$42

Some wines smell like fruit, some wines smell like oak, and some wines just smell. Here's a wine that smells like people. But they're not just people; they're people with pheromones. Musky, spicy, salty . . . And like people the smell is changing – just when you think you've got it olfactorily nailed it's morphed into something else. That's what makes this a sensual chardonnay. Add to that the silky, slippery and slightly sour texture and you've got a New Zealand chardonnay that, if we had a more prudish government, could well have an import ban placed on it.

INCIDENTALS Here's some classic wine-bore information for you. The place where this wine comes from is not called a place; it's called a region. Waipara. It's carefully chosen for its 'protected aspect', which despite its proximity to a ski resort (Mount Hutt) is not 'frost affected' – thanks to the 'moderating maritime influence' of Pegasus Bay. This is how wine people speak all the time.

DROMANA ESTATE Mornington Peninsula Chardonnay 2001
$26

With an aroma of crispy rice, marzipan, wheatgerm, lecithin and garden lime, this classy and pretty sexy chardy runs the rich yet taut gauntlet with a stylish come-hither athleticism and some well-understated panache. Clean citrus flavours spring from the lean acidity which cuts through and keeps fresh the more fleshy and buxom elements. Nectarine, stone fruits, and even a hint of something distantly tropical. A well-educated dusky maiden? Cuddly, but not fat?

INCIDENTALS Wild and natural yeast ferments. A winemaker can be anal and put a killer, single-cell yeast in her wine to guarantee fermentation. It gives her a controlled, predictable result. Or she can let the wild yeasts run free. She can throw caution to the wind, quite literally, and let the natural yeasts that inhabit every vineyard and winery have their own way with the wine. It can make a masterpiece or a mongrel. Faith is everything.

TAMAR RIDGE Pinot Gris 2002
$23

This is hardcore wine – strong flavours, strong alcohol, strong opinions and therefore perfectly suited to most wine occasions where boy meets girl. Let's face it, there might as well be some argy-bargy and differences of opinion rather than 'darling'-this and 'darling'-that agreement sessions followed by the inevitable infidelity. It's about R.E.S.P.E.C.T. And this wine demands it. Even the colour can't be pigeonholed: it's grey, it's white, its pink . . . Nor can the smells and tastes be easily categorised: whiff of Drambuie here, trace of rosewater there, some Turkish delight, pear liqueur and a very hygienic person's sweat.

INCIDENTALS Only pinot gris could produce this effect. It's a white wine that really thinks it's a red wine. This explains the strange colours, smells and flavours mentioned above. Please take your time over pinot gris – don't dismiss it with the kind of unthinking abandon that you would some other white-wine variety. It's a strange wine that finds it hard to fit into the world.

PIZZINI Rosetta 2002
$14

Rosetta is a cute name for a rosé, isn't it? It suggests femininity, and it seems so much less tarty than the word 'rosé' . . . Not for Rosetta is the cheap perfume and sweet cleavage of standard Aussie rosé. She's more demure than that. With a translucent colour that cannot be described, the aroma is both white and red at the same time – but probably more white than red. It's grapy and vinous, delicately perfumed with crushed fruits, and ever so slightly nutty. Once tasted, Rosetta slips down the throat with elegant ease and just the right amount of acid and grip. Cool it down and cohabitate.

INCIDENTALS There are two reasons this rosé is so good: the first is that it's made from sangiovese – an Italian grape variety that is more about texture than overt flavour; the second is that it's made by the Pizzinis – a family with Italian blood in their veins and love in their hearts for rosé as a wine style. Such things count.

MEADOWBANK Henry James Pinot Noir 2001
$39

When pinot is really good it is the most seductive grape. It lures people into fine-wine stores to spend their dough, it lures winemakers to waste decades perfecting the imperfectible, and lures wine writers into the crapulous nonsense you've just read. So this wine: there's a rich dark chocolate smell which has been recently molten and has just set around a rich dark cherry; there's a touch of Turkish delight (really good Turkish delight); and the smell of fresh sex. It's a feminine wine best enjoyed in female company.

INCIDENTALS This wine proudly tells us that it is made predominantly from the pinot noir clone known as MV6. Its name might not sound romantic or sexually inspiring, but it sure smells that way. MV6 is arguably the most sexy of the pinot noir clones, especially when compared to other pinot clones: WD40, KY Jelly, Special K, GTV9 . . .

TARRAWARRA Pinot Noir 2001
$48

If you haven't got a date, this wine is a very good substitute. It's rich, deep, a little intriguing, smartly if a little too trendily dressed, nicely proportioned, and – even more amazing – balanced. Doesn't sound possible does it? Well maybe not in people, but it is in wine. We could strip this wine down to all its components and flavours, but it doesn't taste like that. It's a unique 14-per-cent-alcohol wine liqueur; there are integrated flavours and textures – silky, succulent with a grab bag of the finest ripe berries. It's just plain sexy.

INCIDENTALS Pinot noir. A little knowledge is a dangerous thing. Pity the poor pinot connoisseur, who spends years of their life and the greater part of their income searching for that ever-elusive perfect pinot or beatific burgundy. When pinot is great it can be everything life's meant to be – it all comes together and makes sense and that's what keeps people searching. Pinot isn't Buddha, but Buddha is pinot.

D'ARENBERG Laughing Magpie Shiraz/Viognier 2002
$29

Isn't it kookaburras that laugh and magpies that swoop? The d'Arenberg folk may have got their birds wrong but they've got the blend right. This wine positively reeks of spicy cherries, with a hint of nectarine hiding back there as well. There are dusty plums too – slightly sour but perfectly formed. The texture is silky and soft, and playfully gives your throat a little squeeze as it goes down. It's an entertaining wine to sit and sniff but is also very comfortable being quaffed – and quaffing is really what it's all about. If you're both sitting there sniffing wine, you've got a problem.

INCIDENTALS To use a metaphor appropriate to this chapter, some wines are a little like coitus interruptus. They don't really finish as they should. That's where blending can help. The addition of a little of the white grape viognier to this bolshie McLaren Vale shiraz has not diluted this red, it's extended it. If it works, give it a go – as in the bedroom so in the winery . . .

ST HALLETT Gamekeeper's Reserve Grenache Shiraz Mourvedre 2002
$13

It is time to get a bit homoerotic. The St Hallett Gamekeeper's red is a powerful drink – or is that drug? The varieties that go into this blend once made port, and we all know what port does to men . . . Besides, such is the huge velvety and alcoholic strength of this powerhouse wine that it would kill many women. (Then again, that could be your intention . . .) So the next time you've got Bryce, Gavin, Darren and Miles around, try your luck with this potentially gender-bending internal applicant. They'll love it anyway, no matter what the outcome.

INCIDENTALS Apropos the above, what was the gamekeeper actually reserving this product for? It makes you think of the gay version of *Lady Chatterley's Lover – Lord Chatterley's Partner*? Then again, if they'd had more cheap red around like this, then maybe everyone in the novel would have been happy just doing the gardening.

WIRRA WIRRA Church Block Cabernet Shiraz Merlot 2001
$21

This is the red for a quiet night in. Or not so quiet . . . Put on that CD that you and she or you and he or you and he and she etc etc call *yours.* Set the volume to low, extinguish the electric lamps, light the candles, mix a stiff gin and tonic, cook a roast chicken and a chick pea salad, sit down at the table, listen, laugh and look into each other's eyes, and unthinkingly drink this red wine – all cinnamon, nutmeg, bitter chocolate, liquorice, potter's clay, mud wrestling, rabbits freshly killed, Redskins, cherries, vintage port . . .

INCIDENTALS Wirra Wirra typify the evolution of Australian wine style. Without losing a sense of their region (McLaren Vale's renowned for rich, ripe, porty reds), they've pursued a more savoury course. Let us remind you: children like sweet things, grown-ups like savoury things; so if a winery wants to sell its wine to consumers who can legally buy it, they should make it savoury.

CASCABEL Shiraz Fleurieu 2001
$32

If you took some ripe, roadside plums, some well-worn leather belts and a pinch of allspice, then cooked this strange concoction up in a big cast-iron pot, stirring it occasionally with a polished French-oak spoon, you'd have – once it had cooled down to about 16 degrees centigrade – an approximation of this wonderful wine. But the texture could not be mimicked. It's silky-cum-savoury; there's a gentle yet gruff brush of suede; there's smoothness too as it draws its way lovingly towards your tonsils . . .

INCIDENTALS It's odd how a new region can have the freedom to break away from format winemaking techniques that can so plague and hamstring other older regions. The Fleurieu Peninsula is south of McLaren Vale and has started to produce some very earthy, savoury and deliciously drinkable reds. Cascabel not only makes wine from this region, but also sticks stubbornly to its own vision and path.

KANGARILLA ROAD Shiraz 2001
$19

Men often refer to sensual drinks crudely as 'leg openers' – the theory being that such drinks only exist for, well, you know what . . . Non-men, let's call them women, aren't so vulgar. In fact, leg opening is often the last thing on their minds. Non-men want men to open their mouths and minds and loosen their tongues – to talk. And for that, this is just the product. It's seductively smooth and soft, but it's still a real, almost hairy-chested, red. There's luscious blackberry and polished furniture in the first stanza, all attractive and slippery. And then in the second half a more manly savouriness swaggers in. This wine is not another one of your gay friends . . . Good luck!

INCIDENTALS Perhaps this wine's greatest seductive feature is its drinkability. After all, alcohol can only be an elixir of love if you drink enough of it. With one foot in an older, richer soft style of Australian shiraz, and the other foot in the more savoury modern end, it's dangerous in mixed company.

ST HALLETT Faith Shiraz 2001
$21

The sensuality in this wine stems from three things: its easy drinkability; its Barossan voluptuousness and generosity; and – this might sound contradictory – its relatively low alcohol of 13 per cent. This is what brings a Barossan red into sensual territory: alcohol that entices and excites you rather than groping, ravaging and clubbing you over the head . . . Deeply coloured with aromas to match, this red smells of violets transmogrifying into dark chocolate. Tastes of mulled wine add to the seductive power, yet this is not a lumpy, pudgy product. Like an enjoyable evening, the beginning and end are not defined, but the overall effect is long and satisfying.

INCIDENTALS For once a back label gets it right. We tasted this wine and thought seduction (not in respect of each other, of course); we drank it over lunch then happened to notice the back label: 'These seductive flavours marry with dark chocolate, plum, and cherry to create a balanced wine with great length and flavour.' They suggest cellaring for three to five years, but that's when their wheels fell off. Drink it now with someone you love – or someone you are about to.

HARDYS Tintara Shiraz 1999
$49

Sensual, seductive and svelte, Tintara suggests firm but plentiful masculinity from the very moment you grip the bottle – it's a big, heavy one, too, so you will need both hands. (If lady wine lovers buy this wine, be sure to get the nice young man from the bottle shop to help you carry it out to the Hyundai . . .) The wine inside the bottle has a sensitive touch though. Smelling of bay leaves, camphor, freshly dubbined boots, and meat marinading in this very wine, you've got a powerfully built red capable of a very gentle and deft touch. And talk about a rich, silky texture; this wine defines it.

INCIDENTALS A wine like this needs to be opened two hours before you serve it; you could also decant it into a jug – or one of those posh 100-dollar wine decanters. Shake the wine around – it is tough enough not to mind. Don't serve it in massive glasses or all you will smell is alcohol. Use regular-sized stemware, as wineglasses are nowadays called . . .

METALA Black Label Langhorne Creek Shiraz 2000
$55

If you're on the pull, price is never an issue – or it shouldn't be. Indeed, if you've bought this book in order to find sensual wines with which to ply your trade, well, you won't have even noticed the 55-dollar Metala price-tag. This is no slippery-slidy sweetened-up Ribena love drug. It's a conquering wine – in the mould of Clint Eastwood, Jack Nicholson or Woody Allen (?). With some strange savour and bitter olives, bay leaves and reduced concentrated fruit, it really means business. It's plush but not lush; there's a soy sauce kind of sourness that cuts in three-quarters of the way through. Cook your best lamb shanks, light two candles, put fresh sheets on the bed, open this, and give it a red-hot go.

INCIDENTALS If conversation wanes on this date we've created for you, don't despair. There's almost a 1500-word essay on the front and back labels of this wine. You can learn fascinating stuff about the Metala vineyard in Langhorne Creek, South Australia, and then test each other's reading comprehension.

SENSUAL WINES

PEGASUS BAY Riesling 2002
$29

This is full-on seduction wine. It's late evening – daylight-saving time. You've come back from the beach after having a quick plunge. You're sitting out on a wooden-decked veranda still wrapped in beach towels. The sun is going down and you're at the start of something *really* special. This wine will do its job without you having to think about it. But we have to, so here it is: pavlova topped with kiwi fruit, some really ripe nectarines and a hint of exquisitely made marmalade. It's sweet, yet balanced; unctuous, yet more-ish; honeyed, healthful and supremely sensual.

INCIDENTALS Yes this is a sweet riesling. The grapes were left hanging out on the vines late into the autumn where they intensified their flavour and sweetness. Full-blown, heavily scented flowers attract birds; seed-bursting, skin-splitting ripe fruits do a similar job; so it's no wonder that a ripe rich riesling like this one should help Mother Nature in her quest to continue the species . . .

MARGAN Botrytis Semillon 2002
$22 (375 ml)

Marmalade is a smell and flavour often associated with good sticky wines. This Margan product has it, and that's one of the reasons we like it. But vinified marmalade is only half the battle when making botrytised wines. A good sticky needs the length and balance that remnant acid offers. Margan's got that, too. Dried apricots, varnish, dates, surfboard resin (no, Greg has not been surfing today . . .), and honeyed tea. These flavours linger in a polite manner before some kumquat kicks in, and the acid too. Good with stinky blue cheese.

INCIDENTALS These wines are expensive – for $22 you're only getting a half a bottle – but they are labour intensive. In this instance the poor winemaker had to go through the vineyard and cut half of the fruit-laden vines to dry out the grapes as he watched the other half of the crop slowly rot on the vine, before hand-picking the gooey muck and turning it into wine. Good end result though.

CHAPTER FIVE
UNKNOWN WINES

Chapter Five
UNKNOWN WINES

Bottles of wine can be a little bit like postcards. They pop up all over the world and draw attention to the place from where they have come. But it goes further than that.

As the bottled postcard is consumed, something mysterious happens to you; insidiously, the drinker's mind is filled with notions of the wine's birthplace and upbringing.

This has been happening to Mandy and Rohan. They've been drinking some great central Victorian reds and some unbelievably tasty and affordable north-east Victorian fortifieds – wines that eventually enticed them to spend long-weekend breaks at those places. Some really good riesling and shiraz from Denmark in WA has inspired them in the next holidays to visit Bernadette, Mandy's old school friend who has moved over there, become a lesbian and built herself a *yurt*.

But before this, the first stop on their 'must see' list has been decided by the increasingly delicious Tasmanian pinot they've been splurging on. Ro has in fact become obsessed (you would never have guessed that, would you?); he's even thinking about applying for a job down there . . . 'Don't you think we should do a weekend visit first, darling?' asks Mandy, a little facetiously.

As usual, Rohan fails to see Mandy's ever so subtle irony; he books a five-day weekend on the new *Spirit of Tasmania*. The Spirit is better than they expected but on arrival they're dispirited. Devonport is not a good introduction to Tassie's rare beauties. Mandy makes a mental note to write to the Tasmanian Tourism Commission to suggest that they either make the *Spirit of Tasmania* arrive at a prettier port or blow up Devonport and rebuild it.

Our couple have never been to Tasmania but they have been to the Yarra Valley. From that trip they learned that the thing to do first is stop in at the local pub and find out – via the barmaid – what goes on in the region. (If you want to know what's good in a wine region, ask the bar staff; if you want misinformation and a culture of ever-positive recommendation, go to the tourist office . . .) In the pub in the Yarra Valley they found out what sort of grape varieties the region did best, which wineries had the best cellar doors, and where the good local restaurants and takeaways were. It is like doing a bit of homework, which can help to make the trip more worthwhile. If a region is flooded with pinot noir, for instance, it pays not to spend your holiday hunting down cabernet. There's not a lot of forgiveness shown to people who go to Tassie and ask to try the local tawny port. They're in the wrong region. 'Go north, turn left, stop at the Barossa . . . ' they'll be told by the otherwise helpful cellar-door staff.

So, with this plan in mind, Rohan heads into the nearest pub. Devonport is not the Yarra Valley however. A couple of Boags-soaked loggers object to Rohan's Greenpeace fleece and he nearly gets his head punched in. In fact, Rohan only escapes with his head intact because he manages to convince the angry chainsaw operators that he is actually one of them – a pro-logging spy who is trying to infiltrate the greenies and find out where their next 'action' is. While they slowly digest this information Rohan makes his getaway, Mandy floors the Barina and they head out of Devonport. Fortunately it doesn't take long . . .

Pretty soon they are cruising through the sorts of rural towns and quaint places they've always imagined Tassie to be full of: Deloraine, Westbury, Hagley, Carrick . . . They stop in a pub just outside Launceston where they attempt to get information without violence. This time they are successful. The barmaid is the daughter of one of the local grape growers and they get the lowdown on everything.

Four days later we find the Barina back in Devonport, stacked to bursting point with bottles; M & R are about to board the boat back to Melbourne. They've visited vineyards and cellar doors of labels they know, but they've also discovered a few really good bottles they've never heard about. Mandy and Rohan are relaxed and happy, and have had a great time. But better still, they now hold an indelible mental picture of the places where those luscious pinots they love so much are born, and once they're back in their flat (sorry, *apartment*) in Melbourne, that mental picture somehow makes those pinots taste even better . . .

CASCABEL Tempranillo Graciano 2001
$40

unknown winner

Australia needs more wine like this – much more. From a hand-tended, unirrigated, small vineyard run by a husband-and-wife team, this wine and its winemakers are not about volume or glitzy notoriety – they're just making what they like to drink and what they want to make. This pithy, cherried, dry red is like the blood of the vine: its tannins are earthy, its texture dry and powdery, and its effect is immensely satisfying. Bring on more stuff like this – please . . .

INCIDENTALS Tempranillo? Graciano? Both are Spanish red-wine varieties: the former is grown mainly in the north-east and is a bit like a cross between pinot noir and shiraz. Graciano is what we call grenache, but in the Spanish style it tends to have less raspberry and more earth. The back label talks of 'stony, well-drained soil and forceful gully winds in warm dry summers . . . ' Sounds like Spain; it's actually McLaren Vale.

BROWN BROTHERS Patricia Pinot Chardonnay Brut 1997
$39

Glowing lemony gold, this fizz looks mature, as if it's had some time to contemplate life – and it has. At six years of age (that's 46 in champagne years) Patricia is a mature and strongly opinionated lady. The sterner and firmer pinot noir grapes from Brown Brothers high-altitude Whitlands vineyard come to the fore. They drive the quince and pear liqueur flavours and the pear-skin textural bitterness along a determined path. Patricia demands food.

INCIDENTALS The Brown Brothers' boys are the first in Australia to name a sparkling wine after their mum. Plenty of winemakers have named their sparkling wines after themselves (Pirie, Croser, Dom Perignon . . .) so it's nice to see a little less ego and a bit of maternal respect on the label of a bottle of wine.

YARRABANK Thibaut & Gillet Cuvée 1998
$35

If you're looking for a budget, poncy, yet irrefutably classy bottle-fermented product, something very much in the champagne mould – this is it. With acidity to purse the lips of the very prim and proper, this flavour signature continues all the way through your mouth – a bit like sour Granny Smiths, but attractively so. It's a bubbly that begs for a canapé. Throw in smells straight from the dairy too: really chilled cream, a bit of vanilla... And a steady, subtle effervescence. There's surprising richness in the mouth that narrows, teardrop-shaped, to a fine point at the back of the mouth. Bang on masculine bubbly.

INCIDENTALS Masculine? Yes, the French – as you know – see everything in gender terms: the car (*la voiture*), the garden (*le jardin*), the house (*la maison*), and wine (*le vin*). This bubbly – thanks to the fact that it hasn't gone through malolactic fermentation (see Glossary) is definitely *le fizz*: all firmness and masculine grip.

LANSON Black Label Champagne
$55

There's no cynical sugaring with Black Label. It's extremely dry champagne with an aroma of a dusty, old agricultural museum complete with slightly deteriorating exhibits: an old apple press, an antique nutcracker . . . The bubbles in the wine are better than you'd expect: they're fluffy not firm, and sumptuously creamy; they seem to propel the champagne out of the glass. The flavour is all Granny Smith apple – just like malic acid, and the texture tastes like those same apples' skins.

INCIDENTALS Buying name champagnes is safe but it can sometimes be very boring. Here's a champagne house that has all the legitimacy and history (it was founded in 1760) but through bad distribution and marketing has (until recently) only attracted a cult following. That's good though. It means it's one of the better-value bubblies doing the rounds of the posh wine precincts.

KNIGHT Granite Hills Riesling 2002
$19

Like those people who carry their weight so well that you actually don't notice they're big – or fat – this taut, finely structured riesling hides its 13.5 per cent alcohol very well. There are some real bonuses here – flavours and textures not found in the average riesling: a hint of lavender, some really lovely mandarin with a trace of its pithiness, and a soft, feminine acidity. This is a riesling with curves – in all the right places. Better still, this unknown wine comes from Macedon, the hilly, occasionally snowy bit just an hour north of Melbourne – a region you can call your own.

INCIDENTALS The man who makes this wine, Llew Knight, is a firm believer in hand-picking grapes. He's done tests on different batches of riesling fruit, picking it by machine and then picking other bits of it with his bare hands. He's convinced that bare hands rule. Riesling's delicacy and tendency to spoilage demands such care.

LITTLES Reserve Hunter Valley Semillon 2001
$18

'A beautiful, clear and pure wine, with a bit of oomph' is how Ben described this semillon when asked. Greg replied: 'Yeah, it's no pushover either; it's got a rather stern personality.' We thought about it for another 10 minutes. It has the paradoxical lightweight intensity for which really good semillon is renowned. There's also lemon butter, fresh green herbs, and a hint of cold rosehip tea. Then there's just a trace of phenolic grip – phenols being the gruff, textural bits you get from white grape skins – which only adds to its charm.

INCIDENTALS This is a pretty good example of the fantastic discoveries you can make when visiting – even by the means of your local wine store – a wine region's lesser known wineries. This handsomely packaged product popped up among 30 or so serious semillons one Monday morning while we were tasting for this ridiculous book, and we really loved it.

PALANDRI Sauvignon Blanc 2002
$20

Sauvignon blanc is nicely on display here – a sauv blanc as clear as water. When such wine is so coloured it builds automatic confidence in these two certified sauv blanc haters. The colour lets you know that the wine isn't old or over-ripe or wooded or worked to buggery in the winery. None of those pox overblown tropical/toxic notes are present. Salty preserved lemon aromas remind you more of semillon than SB. It is at the citric end of the ship. A squeeze of lime; slaty minerality on the midriff; drying, narrowing acidity . . . This would go really well with big, juicy Pacific oysters.

INCIDENTALS When Palandri first opened – or should that read *launched* – we were a little sceptical. Too much money, too many dodgy investors; too much hype and bullshit, and far too much lavished on the media event – we know, we were there on a freebie . . . The winemaker, Tony Carpentis, has often produced the goods, however. Good luck to him.

SHADOWFAX Adelaide Hills Sauvignon Blanc 2002
$19

At first you might think there is not much going on with this wine. You know – 'Hey, this is sauv blanc! Why isn't it attacking me and hurting me?' The Shadowfax sauv blanc has self-esteem; it doesn't need to be loud to be noticed. Quality talks; it's almost sotto voce: herbs and fresh bouquet garni (nothing dried out); rosemary and lemon thyme; a trace of tightly wound guava – as if the fruit is marooned on a distant tropical island; and an ethereal texture that acts to dry out the wine, leaving balanced pH, not bitterness and sourness.

INCIDENTALS The bloke who makes this wine is a bespectacled Kiwi who likes rugby and wine. Typical modern New Zealander really . . . He is actually quite skilful – at winemaking – and like a young and talented film director, has a very clear vision, or at least notion, of the wine he wants to make. His siblings are musicians, however. Much more talented . . .

VAVASOUR Marlborough Sauvignon Blanc 2002
$20

While this wine might be a little bit of an unknown, the region from whence it comes – *Mawlbraa* – isn't. In the wine world, New Zealand means sauvignon blanc; Marlborough is its epicentre. This year's Vavasour returns to the same kind of form as the 2000. Initially the wine hints at ripe gooseberry richness, but as soon as you get it in your mouth the acid screams out and speeds the wine through your mouth, cornering sharply. Its texture takes on a mineral salts and pleasantly drying, mouth-puckering quality. It's intense but it's not loud.

INCIDENTALS We said that Marlborough was the epicentre for sauvignon blanc. Indeed, since the 1970s when the first vines penetrated the soil, sauvignon blanc has covered the valley like a noxious weed. The citizens have all grown rich from it, land prices have soared and if the inhabitants of Blenheim (its capital) were just a little bit grateful they'd have a giant sauv blanc grape in the town square.

CRAGGY RANGE WINERY Martinborough Sauvignon Blanc 2002
$20

We presumed this wine would be a lot more money than it is. The bottle is worth $20 alone – it's one of those heavy jobs that are very dangerous to place too vigorously on a glass-topped coffee table. One thing is for sure, the bottle is certainly doing a good job nurturing this fantastic sauvignon blanc. It's deeply scented with smells of musk, honeydew, limes and hothouses with the sprinkler systems on. The floral and vegetal exotica continue inside your mouth where they combine to create a seductively textural wine that almost makes us think we've got this bottle in the wrong chapter . . .

INCIDENTALS On top of the expensive bottle, in this wine you're getting the juice of a single vineyard – in this case the Te Muna Road vineyard. It's been hand-harvested, at 11 different times (in wine-bore verbiage the fruit from these different times is called a parcel) and given the finest upbringing possible. Again we wonder at the price. Could it be a typo?

GEMBROOK HILL Yarra Valley Chardonnay 2001
$28

This little-known Yarra Valley producer is boutique winemaking at its best. A bit of land, a few vines, a year's work and here you have it – drinkable high-quality, characterful chardonnay. Its finest quality is restraint and a dry laconic manner. This is not a chardonnay berating you, in an American accent, with its CV. It's self-assured, doesn't need to brag and, like all good chardonnay, its keen acid structure provides the flavour and personality: there's a taste of a salt lick, spice, nettles . . .

INCIDENTALS Greg first discovered Gembrook Hill on a restaurant wine list. A lot of boutique wineries rely not so much on wine-store sales but on what is termed 'on-premise' sales. They sell them to restaurants. Some restaurants like unknown wines, the logic being that customers won't have heard of them, won't know the wines' true retail price, and will happily pay the cynical mark-up Mr Restaurateur charges . . .

TIN COWS Chardonnay 2001
$22

In many ways we think this is the typical bistro/brasserie/tapas bar/wine-bar chardonnay. It's chardy through and through, but it's in the new Australian style. There's nothing broad, fat or overtly alcoholic about the flavour, texture or speed of this wine. It's not the buxom blonde – thank God. It's more athletic: high cheekbones, short hair with a natural wave, and toned legs. Chilled cream and stainless-steel aromas, the slightest waft of lemon . . . The texture is silky and syrupy with sharper, more defined edges. Tin Cows finishes with a mineral-water tang. One bottle/two people – no drama.

INCIDENTALS When Tarrawarra, the owners of the Tin Cows label, purchased the land on which they planted the vines for Tin Cows, Greg was a bit bemused. It was a particularly wet season and the Tin Cows vineyard looked like a swamp. The success of this wine proves three things: 1. Chardonnay can grow anywhere. 2. You can never judge the quality of land by one visit alone. 3. Gregory should not go into vineyard consultancy.

TRINITY HILL Shepherds Croft Hawkes Bay Chardonnay 2001
$23

This chardonnay entrances. You can waste days trying to work out exactly what it smells like. There are so many things: nettles, vanilla custard, breadfruit, green figs, hazelnut, and trifle made with double sherry. In fact, you expect it to be a lot richer than it is. But this chardonnay doesn't descend into flabland; it's tightly held within a minerally frame, which makes its finish almost start at the beginning. It's effortless to drink – and rewarding. If this indicates the future style of New Zealand chardonnay, the Southern Hemisphere will be a better place.

INCIDENTALS Talk to any Kiwi who is into their wine and they'll tell you that Hawkes Bay (the home of this wine) is New Zealand's premium red-wine area. They'll crap on about the 'brulliant' merlot and cabernet sauvignon that is 'pucked' from Hawkes Bay vines. In good seasons it's true, but the chardonnay is often better. Chardonnay is the blackberry of the vitus family, and it will grow anywhere.

MEADOWBANK Pinot Noir 2002
$28

Here's another 750 millilitres of reasons to spend some money on Tasmanian pinot noir. For the amount of depth and intensity you get, it is a bargain. Pinot growers on the mainland would struggle for years to get this result, poor bastards. And the Meadowbank also does that weirdo pinot thing – running a fine line between acid and fruit; between plushness and austerity; feral animal skins and fresh berries; bitter herbs and sweet spice . . . While it is not the silliest pinot going around at present, it is very much a kiddie and it will improve in the velvet stakes over the next few months.

INCIDENTALS Blending of regions. In places like Tassie, the weather is incredibly variable; it can rain in one place and yet be sunny a few kilometres down the road. This is where the people at Meadowbank have got it sussed – drawing the grapes from the Coal River Valley (east of Hobart) and the Derwent Valley (south of Hobart). It's a two-way bet, and they usually win.

PEGASUS BAY Pinot Noir 2001
$52

The intense ruby colour of this pinot could fool you into thinking it's not pinot at all; but stick your nose in the glass and there's no denying its authenticity. Low-yielding, struggling, weatherbeaten vines make for tough, dark skins – that's where the colour comes from. There are aromas of black cherries from an old, obscure (and probably defunct) variety, and it reminds us of blood on gravelly dirt. What really powers this wine however are the abundant, velvety, yet drying tannins. It has guts, class and maybe even an ability to bottle age – if you're into that sort of thing.

INCIDENTALS This wine comes from Waipara, the region just north of Christchurch on New Zealand's South Island, and is made by the wine-mad Donaldson family. Mr and Mrs Donaldson got the kids into wine. Now one of the kids, Matthew, makes it with his winemaker wife, and Edward, his brother, markets it. Wine keeps families together . . .

SHADOWFAX K Road Sangiovese Merlot Shiraz 2001
$25

A pretty inspired blend this one, all of the characters in this triumvirate are doing their bit. Sangiovese is supplying the drying grip, merlot a few buxom curves, and shiraz some spicy language. K Road is obviously a happening place. The best thing about this wine however, and indeed without which it would be a disaster, is the integration of the three grape berry products. It's a good blend. They're all getting on. Shiraz comes on stage first, then merlot appears for a couple of numbers and sangiovese finishes the show. And it rocks.

INCIDENTALS Blending. This blend is no accident. The winemaker didn't have bits of merlot, shiraz and sangiovese in the back paddock and just pick them and chuck them together. Along with the shiraz he had in his own Werribee vineyard, the winemaker 'carefully sourced parcels' of merlot and sangiovese from the Adelaide Hills. Then he chucked them together . . .

JANE BROOK Back Block Shiraz 2001
$20

There's a lot of value here in this slightly weird, savoury and faintly Spanish wine. The first thing you'll notice is the smell: pastrami, deli counters, parsnip, Barbecue Shapes, fish emulsion . . . All of that is backed up by a grainy, textural mouthful of spicy shiraz. Big lumps of powdery tannin provide some rustic honesty, but pure fruit flavours of cassis and satsuma plums counterbalance and give a clean, long and clear structure. This is an uplifting, intriguing wine, which changes in the glass all the bottle through. It isn't wine-factory robot juice; it's a living thing. Greg has consumed three bottles of this wine and still likes it. Amazing.

INCIDENTALS This wine comes from the Swan Valley just outside of Perth. It's not a trendy wine region; it's stinking hot and mostly flat. Likewise, Jane Brook is no new architect-designed winery; it's an old, established wine label which achieved a degree of fame with fortified wine – notably white port. A new lady winemaker is now in charge. She is clearly a rock star.

CHEVIOT BRIDGE Shiraz 2001
$25

Some people love sweet things; they gravitate like bees towards sticky, gluey, tacky food. Then there are the Vegemite eaters of the world – the salt and savoury lovers. If you're the latter, this is your wine. This shiraz is at the pepper, bush raspberry and nearly-ripe-blackberry end of the flavour spectrum. Yet that's just one facet; the really appealing thing is the texture. This wine grips you in a close embrace – the tannins are so fine and effortless, no surface is left uncovered. The flavour and texture remain like a long autumnal shadow cast over the end of an otherwise perfect day.

INCIDENTALS If you drive up the Hume Highway from Melbourne, one of the first turnoffs you'll get to is Tallarook. From here you'll eventually get to the Yea Valley. That's where this wine comes from. It's boring country to look at as you whiz past at 110 kilometres per hour, but the soil and the climate have the potential to make some great wine.

SCORPO Mornington Peninsula Shiraz 2001
$32

Not everyone will like this wine. But it wasn't made with silly democratic appeal in mind. It has its own personality and thank God for that. It's a bit pongy – leaking septic tanks, swamps, and brackish, marshy land. Fish wouldn't live in it. But on top of that there's some very bright pepper, freshly crushed and sprinkled over barely ripe berries. Some goat is roasting in the oven and it's covered in pepper too . . . A blueberry tart is cooling on the bench . . . After a few glasses you don't seem to smell the septic any more . . . A drying and savoury structured wine.

INCIDENTALS And a relatively expensive wine, too, we agree; but to get the grapes ripe the Scorpos had to carefully nurture each vine, pruning off excess bunches, cutting off leaves and generally frigging about so that every grape got its best chance to see the ever-fickle Mornington Peninsula sun.

FERNGROVE Dragon Shiraz 2001
$25

Wine types bang on about the brilliance of Frankland River – the place where this red comes from. A lot of the stuff we taste is a bit, well, it seems they're still practising . . . Ferngrove's Dragon has shown the region's potential, however. This is a wine with a lot of polish and subtle sophistication. It smells like the brand-new wooden dash on a Jaguar, complete with some fine leather upholstery on the seats. And a little bit of berry-scented car cologne – you know, that stuff you can buy from Auto Bahn . . . A herbal taste controls your mouth, with rosemary and thyme kicking in, but it's smooth and very well integrated. It made us long for some roast lamb.

INCIDENTALS Some winemakers have love–hate relationships with their mothers-in-law – we all do, at least those of us so terribly lucky to be married . . . This wine was lovingly named after the winemaker's mother-in-law. Yes, Shiraz is a funny pet name, isn't it?

UNKNOWN WINES | 159

SHADOWFAX McLaren Vale Shiraz 2001
$35

There's been a lot of love put into this wine. The deep, dense, dark colour is the first thing you notice. The wine looks bulletproof. Then the smell combines herbs, spices, powdered dark chocolate, fertile dry earth and a hint of gumleaf. Or is that bay leaf? To drink it is a very pleasant exercise in tannin anger management. This wine has a sort of seamless suppleness – flesh and skeleton are one. It would be really good at yoga but it's no tofu eater. This is beef city. It is firm but fair, and the second half of the bottle rocks.

INCIDENTALS When a wine like this has been so well made and offers such great drinking pleasure, well . . . drink it now. The winemaker reckons 'it will age superbly over the next four to five years'. Our only problem with this advice is the adverb. We think it is drinking *superbly* now. But if you must cellar . . .

HOWARD PARK Scotsdale Great Southern Shiraz 2001

$34

This super-premium, screw-capped shiraz called Scotsdale, from the Howard Park winery in Western Australia, sits at one extreme end of the Australian-shiraz scale. At the other end you'll find Wolf Blass and other rich, sweet, warm-climate reds. As you've probably guessed, Scotsdale shares none of these characteristics: it's savoury, svelte, Schezuan-peppery and smoky. In fact there's a real après-bushfire, delicately charred fauna taste and smell to this wine. You've been warned. But we reckon it is very, very drinkable.

INCIDENTALS Great Southern. No, it's not Antarctica or a golf course. This rather vague name refers to the large wine region on the southern tip of Western Australia, around the towns of Denmark and Albany. It's cooler down there and the fruit from these vineyards reflects that climate. And for shiraz it rocks.

UNKNOWN WINES

GARRY CRITTENDEN 'i' Nebbiolo 2000
$25

Tannins, aniseed, celery, salt, game – but not so much hung game as fresh bunnies. Pale to off-rose in colour, with those burnt, brown rim edges that nebbiolo is renowned for, this red has a cleansing acidity that does the full-flush treatment in your mouth. After each gobful you want another one, and another bite of food, and another gulp of wine . . . The flavour is round and a little rich, which will satisfy both nebbiolo addicts and industrial-style red quaffers. You can find more in this wine as it morphs in the glass: rose prunings, cinnamon, cologne . . . But it's the tannins at the very end that do it: long, dry and chalky.

INCIDENTALS The Crittenden lads – dad Garry and son Rollo – have been messing about with Italian varietals for a few years now. Good wine does take time; but they've done a great job in advocating the long-term worth of these wines. Now they've got the real deal with this nebbiolo.

SUMMERFIELD Cabernet 2001
$30

One of the really good things about small wineries is that there's no passive-aggressive 'brand manager ' in the company to censor things – the wine style or the back label. Individuals and their vineyards are allowed to express their personality and when they're on song it all rocks like a baby in a cradle. This western Victorian cabernet, from the Pyrenees region, has got the iron-ore-like tannic grip typical of cab savs of this area, but it has well-married oak spice and great blackberried fruit depth. It's full-on but nonetheless it's very attractive. Once again, we recommend this cheaper standard label to its more expensive reserve product.

INCIDENTALS The winemaker reckons that along with the berry flavours in this wine there's also some molasses. Molasses? Yes, dead right. Where do you get molasses from in red wine? Like sugarcane, it comes from sun and fire; in this case, really ripe fruit and charred oak.

CHAPTER SIX
UNPRONOUNCEABLE WINES

Chapter Six
UNPRONOUNCEABLE WINES

Mandy has been reading some fairly heavy wine literature. There are countless books about wine and most of them deal with French wines and how brilliant they are – French wines that are so brilliant no one can afford to drink them.

Mandy is reading one of these very books tonight, and while Rohan snores gently by her side, she burns into her brain such scintillating facts as the establishment of the 1855 Bordeaux Classification System. This was a process, she discovers, whereby a bunch of Napoleon III's mates and some Bordeaux wine brokers formalised a five-tiered wine-classification system of the 61 leading wines of Bordeaux. Mandy has never tasted any of these wines, but she rather likes the whole idea of classifying things . . . It makes everything so clear; you then know what is good and what is bad.

Mandy applies the 1855 Bordeaux Classification System to other things in her life: CDs, films, friends, shopping precincts, cosmetics, TV newsreaders . . .

Rohan's Deep Purple CDs are obviously ignoble and therefore not classified; his U2 Greatest Hits CD she rates as a Second Growth – to use the Bordeaux parlance. She's been listening to Norah Jones a lot lately and thinks she is incredible; she is ranked First Growth. When it comes to friends, the system works perfectly. Mandy's Sydney friend, Sasha Saccaciai (the $250,000-a-year, 5-foot-eight, 49-kilogram fashion buyer), is obviously First Growth; while Ro's ex-girlfriend Theresa Talbot (a physiotherapist with whom he is still on good terms (it was one of those happy, mutual break-ups) just sneaks into Fourth Growth. (Theresa is from a very wealthy, well-connected family . . .)

Mandy starts doing this classifying thing everywhere. It really starts to annoy Ro – particularly the classification of Jessica Rowe, the Channel Ten newsreader. 'She is so not First Growth, Mandy! She is *vin de table*! And when can we start drinking these Bordeaux wines, Mandy? Isn't that the point?'

These kinds of comments always shit Mandy. She plans to buy some Bordeaux, but she's not going to drink it with Rohan. On a weekend trip to Sydney to visit Sasha, she splurges on a bottle of Château Cos d'Estournel. It's a Second-Growth Bordeaux. (Sasha is always on about how much she is into French wine . . .) Sasha has also lined up some serious shopping with First-Growth Prada handbags and Second-Growth Gucci accessories. Lunch on Saturday is at a Third-Growth Italian restaurant; Saturday night is a First-Growth private party with Grand Cru synthetic drugs and Fifth-Growth emasculated Sydney single men . . . It's a classifier's dream. The whole weekend is definitely Premier Cru.

Maybe the economy-class plane trip was symbolic of the weekend's tone. Sasha insists they open the d'Estournel before they go out for lunch; the wine tastes metallic and hard; Sasha's mobile won't stop ringing; other friends stop by; lunch is brought forward; the wine could have been a 15-dollar bottle of Australian cabernet and no one would have known . . . and why do Sydney men all have the same haircut and wear the same sort of shirt? The drugs help, but one thing keeps bothering Mandy – why didn't the 200-dollar wine sing? Maybe it's the occasion?

Mandy gets home on Sunday evening disappointed, disillusioned and pondering it all. She realises that there is one anomaly in the Bordeaux Classification System and her own classification systems. All new CDs are about the same price – no matter which 'growth' she has assigned them. Films are all the same entry price, no matter how good or bad they are. The poncy 61 wines of Bordeaux, however, have had their prices set by the wine brokers back in 1855. Why? In order to make money. In a flash of insight she understands. *It is all inherently evil.*

Sunday-night dinner is a Rohan Minute Steak and some Guigal Côtes du Rhône red – a wine a tenth of the price of the d'Estournel. The d'Estournel might have enjoyed Ro's company more, but that didn't matter now. The journey into the wines of Bordeaux and its evil classification system was a rich-woman's sport. Mandy thinks she might leave that up to Sasha . . .

'LA GOYA' Manzanilla
$12 (375 ml)

Manzanilla is pale dry sherry. It's best served cold and is fantastic with little dead fish things. This one is a tangy, nutty, dry, resiny white-wine mutant. We say that because of the way such sherry (manzanilla is sort of related to fino) is made. It's actually very dull, boring white wine that is allowed to go off in a barrel. Only it doesn't go off because a yeast fog forms over the top of the liquid protecting it from oxygen – just like the way a doona protects you from the cold. The result is this wine. Controlled spoilage rocks. Farting under the doona doesn't . . .

unpronounceable winner

INCIDENTALS Sherry comes from a place called Jerez in the sunny, dry south of Spain. It's a fantastic place, with bullfights, flamenco and heaps of cold fino served everywhere. Sherry is called sherry because the idiot Poms who first started importing it couldn't say Jerez (pronounced with a guttural 'h' – *haireth*). Jerez is so much more fun to say.

LA GITANA Manzanilla
$2.50 (187ml), $12 (375 ml), $20 (750 ml)

With an aroma of hazelnuts marinating in nail-polish remover, not to mention smells of window cleaner and old camphor chests, La Gitana isn't really trying to seduce you, unless you're into window-cleaning manicurists. Her charms work slowly, and you gradually have to come to terms with the fact that this is white wine. Weird white wine, but white wine nevertheless. The taste is salty, dry, tangy, resinous, a little piquant, but strangely pure and fresh. It puckers and makes you want to eat and sip and eat and sip and eat and sip . . . It's the liquid equivalent of a plunge into the sea on a hot day.

INCIDENTALS The trick to getting a taste for manzanilla and fino sherries is to get past that first sniff and taste – all the fly spray and nail-polish remover. Just like eating something that is a bit weird, you have to train yourself. Jeffrey Steingarten – The Man Who Ate Everything – reckoned that it took 10 tries before you acquired a taste. This works for every food and drink, except monkeys' brains and verdelho . . .

CARPENÈ MALVOLTI Prosecco di Conegliano
$24

This, as you can probably tell from the bottle shot, is sparkling wine. It is Italian sparkling wine known as Prosecco. Prosecco is like drinking cute bubbly made from Granny Smith apples. The flavour of this one is just like that, but imagine they're sliced up and atop an apple pie, complete with a smidgen of brown sugar and a touch of cinnamon. In fact, this would be a pretty good drink with an apple cake or apple pie. Excellent at about 9 am too. Cute fizz, never scary. It makes you feel happy, which is all wine can ever be asked to do.

INCIDENTALS The prosecco makers of Italy get it at both ends, so to speak. The grapes they use to make prosecco are recycled; the pressed skins and pips then get double-whammied to produce grappa, that machine-oil clear spirit. You can start the day with this drink, too – in your coffee. Grappa or prosecco, anyone? Both?

UMANI RONCHI Villa Bianchi Verdicchio Dei Castelli di Jesi 2001
$12

This wine blew us away with the quality and its low price. Ripe, honeydew melon and lipstick (the generic smell or fragrance of lipstick) precedes a salty, oyster-water and rosewater flavour. God, it is a sensual wine too . . . And the thing that gives away its wogginess is the slight resinousnessnessness in the background. Fortunately the standard Italian hessian bag (or phenolic) textures are at a minimum. The only problem is the vile pale-green plastic cork.

INCIDENTALS Verdicchio gets its name from the yellowish-green colour of the grapes. As a grape vine it's not considered particularly noble; wine tossers don't really rate it. Apparently it has few exciting or distinctive features. But who gives a toss what the tossers think? It's drinkable white wine, and this one rocks. From the Marche region of Italy, by the way . . .

WILLIAM FEVRE Petit Chablis 2001
$27

This reminds us of a cold swimming pool; oh, and mineral water, pool salts, lemon rind and some fresh apple – the Granny Smith variety. A delicate, fresh glassful of clean and gently acidic white wine, it's been given some subtle oomph in the form of a mid- to back-mouth trace of gruffness, as if there's been a hessian bag thrown into the fermenter. The drinkability is high, which means you start to get a bit giddy and imagine even more weirdo flavours and smells: dissolved minerals, shells, freshly shucked oysters eaten straight from the half shell . . . Not a bad food for this wine.

INCIDENTALS Real acidity versus added acid . . . This wine tastes of real or natural acidity. The acid flavour and effect seems so effortlessly interwoven into the whole package; it's not an add-on. The acid isn't overdubbed; it's recorded live, it's organic. It doesn't just clean out your mouth, but revivifies it; there's no 'arghhh' but more often a pleasantly realised 'ahhhh . . . '

RIPAROSSO Montelpulciano d'Abruzzo Illuminati 2000
$11

Some of us know this wine well. A syndicated wine store with the initials 'V' and 'C' has been selling it for a couple of years now. And plenty of it. Indeed, one of the things to recommend this wine is its availability, distribution, and, of course, its price. The twigs and sticks and gruff grape-skin tannins so typical of Italian wine are here to provide the breadth and texture, but there's a denser, riper, almost cooked-berry flavour at the core. It is a good, thoughtless, Sunday BBQ red; or a good and slightly weird second, third or fourth bottle to follow the more ponceforth ones all dinner parties must nowadays begin with. Stones, blood, port and dry liqueur . . .

INCIDENTALS This one is from the Abruzzo region in Italy's east, and Illuminati is considered one of the better producers in an area that's often a little too rustic, if you know what we mean. Montelpulciano is also the grape's name; it makes for spicy, chewy red with drinkable tannins and acidity. This 2000 job is a little more chewy than some, so if you're new to Italian wines, have a go.

ZENATO Valpolicella Superiore 1999
$23

This is the second cracker Valpolicella we've put in this year's guide. So interesting and drinkable and food-friendly are these wines that Greg was heard to comment: 'Shit, they're good; *I'd* buy these wines . . .' Ben wastes most of his income on such wines already – but he's a wine tosser. Yet this Valpolly: grainy. Very grainy. With traces of sour blood and very fine ceramic dust, it does to your mouth what an expensive bio-dio-orgo exfoliating skin treatment does to your outer cutaneous layer – cleanses, revitalises and makes you feel younger. The wine smells like old oak casks and nail-polish remover; it tastes like prune juice and potter's clay. *Allora.*

INCIDENTALS Valpolicella is made from grapes called corvina and rondinella. It comes from the hills around Verona and, well, up there, in the northern part of Italy, the locals are a little different to your standard Italians. They look different, they speak differently, and they reckon Valpolicella is the only red wine in the world to drink. They're wrong, of course, but don't you love that attitude?

SPERI Valpolicella Classico Superiore 2000
$23

Italians often call Valpolicella 'twice-skimmed milk' (or '*latte doppio niente*' as Ben says in his crap Italian). The decaf soy latte of Italian red wine. It's often thin, weedy and a bit shit. But this one isn't. For 23 bucks you're getting Valpolicella red about as good as it gets. It's rich, dark and a bit chocolatey even, with a typically Italian grainy texture and a distant echo of wood and spice. The flavour is sweet and sour and fruit and flesh – rockmelon wrapped in prosciutto – and the finish is a little like sucking on a prune pip. It is incredibly drinkable.

INCIDENTALS Valpolicella is from the north-east of Italy. Its sister is Soave, a remarkable white wine in that it smells and tastes of absolutely nothing. Valpolicella is a cheap red, Valpolicella Classico is a bit better, and Valpolicella Classico Superiore, the best. Superiore also means that it has to have at least one year's ageing in the bottle.

VALDERIZ Ribera del Duero 2000
$24

With a label that looks like it's from some sort of photography exhibition, you know this is a slightly intellectual wine – and the back label reads a bit like an SBS documentary too. This dark wine has the smell of subcutaneous chestnut skin and milled chestnut meal; in fact, it's purpose-made for an autumn day, some roast chestnuts, a roast rabbit and roast parsnip. These far-fetched evocations derive from the tannins – they are everywhere and they are *fine*, as if your mouth is in the eye of a tannin storm, where everything is eerily peaceful.

INCIDENTALS If you taste this wine amidst a few Australian reds, the only thing that will be familiar to you is the distant whiff of dusty oak. Structurally, this wine might as well be from another planet. And it is – Spain. This is what makes it so fantastic – the point of difference. Don't just spend your life sucking on local wine products; go offshore sometimes.

FELSINA BERARDENGA Chianti Classico 2000
$35

The Tuscan countryside comes to the fore in the aromas of this more rustic wogola red: you are walking up to an old stone winery just on dusk, there are cypress trees pointing heavenwards, and there's the slightest smell of blood and bone in the air. There's a cemetery on your left and a fresh, empty grave lies awaiting . . . At the bottom of the grave the clay is wet, while the dug soil lying to one side of the hole is crumbling and crusting. A couple of dogs have been doing their own digging around the base of an old cherry tree. It's a lopsided tree, falling over the dilapidated frame of an old wooden outhouse, the rich, ripe fruits staining the 300-year-old timber . . .

INCIDENTALS Many people think that the above wine writing is 'at best, fanciful'. Our great mate James Halliday said that of one of the reviews in the first *Drink Drank Drunk*. We disagree; we just don't see it James's way; he can write the way he wants, and that has its own value; but, by the same token, we'll stay away from compiling wine encyclopaedias. If reading is more than prescription and instruction, then there's scope for the above review.

RIECINE Chianti Classico 2000
$35

Serious sangiovese with enough oomph and guts to last some distance. A bit sour with some bitter sweetness, the acids are the ingredient that cut through the fruit 'profile', as the wine wankers say. This keeps the wine on its tippy-toes, but it is no way light or poofy. Funny we should say tippy-toes because one of the marked qualities of this chianti is a gracefulness as it glides across the mouth area. In fact, it is Nureyev pulling a pirouette *sur le cou-de-pied* – otherwise known as a very sick ballet move. Texturally the wine is rich yet chalky; there are dry cosmetics, more-ish acidity and purity. Dark chocolate and very well-made cherry liqueur. More please.

INCIDENTALS Take the lid off this wine for a while before you drink it. At initial opening it seems smelly and stifled, like a genie that's been trapped inside a bottle too long. Don't be afraid to open this wine a couple of hours before luncheon. And be prepared to pay it some attention over the course of that luncheon too, as it wafts and wanes through an attractive array of flavours and smells.

CHÂTEAU VILLERAMBERT Julien Minervois 2000
$31

One of the criticisms of red wine from France and Italy by those brought up on Aussie ball-tearers is that they're a bit weak, thin and pissy. No guts. Well, here's one that might change your mind. It comes from a warmer region in the south-west of France near Narbonne and Carcasonne. They have bullfights down here, and more crime and less stuffiness. This wine is primal to smell – all pure, dark and deep grape juice. It is rich in body and velvety to taste; then come the tannins marching in. They dry out the back of your mouth. It is perfect with a cigarette – Gauloise unfiltered . . .

INCIDENTALS Minervois is from the south-west of France. It's an area given to such grapes as cinsault, carignan, shiraz, mourvèdre and grenache. These grapes all have strong personalities and provide plenty of oomph and flavour. Minervois is a bit of a bargain when you consider what you have to pay for all-too-sensitive and elegant Bordeaux reds . . .

GUIGAL Côtes du Rhône 2000
$23

Côtes du Rhône is not that hard to pronounce, so maybe it shouldn't be in this chapter. And it is one of the best reds for weekday drinking going around. But it's here because it's French and it would complain if it weren't. You know how patriotic they are. As for the drink, it's so effortless it's almost not red wine. But it does provide the comforting warmth of red wine and is somehow both old and young at the same time. Although it betrays no signs of age in colour, there's an ever so faint dusty savouriness that finishes the wine off almost in the place of tannin. This is not in-your-face Australian shiraz fruit; it's more muted and subtle. It's Flaubert, not Bryce Courtenay.

INCIDENTALS We mentioned the effortless drinkability in the review above and we weren't fibbing. So effortlessly drinkable is it that having been interrupted as we were reviewing this wine we happened to enter into a very heated discussion on the age of Joan Collins, and drank the lot, much to our professional embarrassment. We had to go to all the trouble of calling in another bottle and pretending the other was corked.

CHÂTEAU DE MONTFAUCON Côtes du Rhône 2000
$25

Here is an affordable and characterful Rhone red. And it smells. These smells come from dodgy yeast infections, old barrels, questionable fruit-handling protocols and a certain *vive-le-lunch* winemaking approach. Who cares about robot winemaking when you can get a fun red like this? Fly spray, wet pepper, fennel and all those smells you get from grapes that have struggled to ripen as they cling to the sides of Rhone Valley slopes. The effect of the wine's strong yet integrated acids suit it to foods like lamb – or *Gigot de Australienne* . . . If you are tossy and eat venison, yeah, it would be good too.

INCIDENTALS The land upon which these grapes are grown has been trod on, farmed and shat upon since Cro-Magnon man and woman walked this earth. Is it any wonder that the same earth produces such interesting flavours in any plant that bothers to bear fruit? This is what the wine tosser word '*terroir*' is all about.

CELLARING VERSUS DRINKING

Is cellaring a waste of time? Mostly the answer is yes. A very great percentage of Australian wines and affordable imported wines are purposefully made and designed to be drunk young. In a way it's a shame that unlike milk and fresh orange juice, wine labels don't carry a use-by date. Although, having said that, legislation has recently been passed in Australia that will require Australian wine labels to carry a 'best before' date. The weird thing is that this is only to comply with food-standard regulations; it has nothing to do with cellaring advice . . .

If we had a dollar for every time we'd drunk either our own, someone else's or some silly winery's dead red, rotten white or 'museum release', we'd be about to buy out Bill Gates – twice. These old wines are the innocent victims of cellaring. And cellaring is perhaps the strangest manifestation, or symptom, of that strangest of all mental illnesses: wine connoisseurship.

What is it about wine and what is it about people that they feel they have to own wine and lock it away in the dark? It's a strange fetish in that it's both sadistic (you're letting the wine die a slow death) and it's masochistic (you're depriving yourself of the pleasure of delicious young wine). Stranger still, when, if at all ever, you do take the wine out of the cellar and drink it, you convince yourself and everyone else that it is superb.

These cellaring sadomasochists fail to understand a simple truism. Cellaring does not improve wines; it simply changes them. The changes are mostly for the worse but in some cases can be if not better then at least interesting.

From the moment the wine is put in the bottle it is dying a slow death on an inevitable course towards vinegar. Cellaring slows up this process but it's still happening. Any flavour that is gained is at the cost of one lost. And basically reds get drier and whites get sweeter.

Still not convinced? If you want to cellar wines you need the following conditions. A cool, dark place with a temperature of around about 12 to 16 degrees Celsius. It can be lower than this but the key thing is that there is little fluctuation. If your 'cellar' temperature spikes and drops the wines follow suit and air can be sucked in through cork as it pistons in and out in the neck of the bottle. This is not a good thing. Humidity can also be a factor: ideally this should be around 60 to 65 per cent. Any lower corks dry out; any higher they get mouldy. We'd be so bold to suggest that these conditions are not found in linen cupboards, on top of fridges or under beds . . .

Given that you're still quite determined to cellar wine, we've put together a list from this year's guide. The wines herein may under certain conditions, in certain climates, under certain circumstances and under the influence of certain planetary actions, given that everything's equal, at the end of the day, and in accordance with, with respect to and with due procedural prudence, change for the better, or something – if you're lucky.

Brown Brothers Riesling 2002
Knight Granite Hills Riesling 2002
Jacob's Creek Reserve Riesling 2001
Orlando Steingarten Riesling 2001
Poet's Corner Henry Lawson Semillon 2001
Tyrrell's Lost Block Semillon 2002
Tahbilk Marsanne 2002
Shaw and Smith M3 Chardonnay 2001
Water Wheel Bendigo Shiraz 2001
Knappstein Shiraz 2001
Mitchelton Central Victoria Shiraz 2001
Metala Black Label (and their ordinary, cheaper white label from most vintages) Shiraz 2000
Hill of Gold Shiraz 2001

EPILOGUE

Here's what the wine industry has noticed about itself lately:

- Australian winemakers squashed a record total of 1.65 million tonnes of grapes in vintage 2002.
- Australia is now sixth in the world ranking in production and fourth in exports.
- There are 90 grape varieties grown commercially in Australia.
- Red grapes account for over 60 per cent of the vineyards in Australia.
- Malbec plantings have decreased.
- There are 188 producers growing malbec.
- There are 1176 producers growing chardonnay.
- There are 62 producers of organic wines.
- There are 1292 wineries with cellar doors.
- Tasmania is the fastest-growing wine region in percentage terms.
- In the past five years nearly three times more shiraz vines have been planted than chardonnay.
- Wine imports account for 4.1 per cent of domestic sales.
- There are over 1600 wine producers and of those only 22 account for 92 per cent of total sales.
- Over the last three years a new wine producer has been born in Australia every 61 hours.

Here's what *we've* noticed about the wine industry this year:
- There's some good cheap merlot.
- Generally, cheap red is better quality than previously.
- Too much chardy!

- Greater divergence of style – shiraz is not always made the same way; there are variations on the theme.
- Not enough straight malbec.
- Better sauvignon blanc, but still plenty of sauvignon bland.
- Crap cheap sparkler (Why not put the crap chardy into the crap sparkler?)
- The dreadful wine-company philosophy that you need a wine in every category – don't make three good wines; make 19 shit ones – it is all about competing in the marketplace and moving product at volume per category to meet perceived needs/features/benefits . . . (No, we don't know what that means either.)
- WA has budget wine!!! Better value and better cheap wine as the years go by.
- Better overall quality in Tassie wine – especially pinot.
- The Barossa is still stuck in a rut; some producers are digging themselves out; others are digging further down – leaving the wheels spinning . . .
- Beware of 2002 Hunter Valley products . . .
- Do not drink verdelho. Stop it now and if you grow it, pull it out before it takes over the world.
- Look out for fantastic value with fortified wine – especially all those Penfolds and Seppelts jobs.
- Stelvins: now there are more on reds as well. At the same time, cork quality – if our stats mean anything – seems to be improving.
- You-beaut-super-premium $$$ wines are never as drinkable as their cheaper stablemates. Drink the 17-dollar shiraz, not the 77-dollar Winemaker's Reserve Estate Select Bin 'Amazing Grace' Shiraz . . .

GLOSSARY

Wine does have its own language but it's not hard to learn. The nouns and adjectives can be weird but fun; for the normal drinker there are not too many technical words to master; and there are some seemingly absurd phrases and bits of jargon that are funny in their ridiculous self-importance and exclusivity.

Nouns (or names to identify things with)

ACID Acid is a natural component of grapes and wine. Getting the acid level right is a critical part of winemaking. There are lots of different acids in wine – they can make a wine refreshing, sharp and piquant.

BALANCE All the components of a wine come together to give it harmony: the fruit, the acid, the alcohol, the tannins, but not necessarily the label . . . Some very nice wines have ugly labels.

BARREL An oak container of 225 litres used by winemakers to ferment and/or mature both red and white wine. Barrels are invariably described as 'new', 'old', 'French' or 'American'. New oak imparts a very strong, dominant flavour; old oak lets the fruit talk; French is spicy; American is sweet.

BOTTLE AGE Wine typically goes through three stages of development. In the first stage it's just fermented grape juice with all its natural aromas and flavours. In the second stage the winemaker fiddles and adds his bits – maybe a bit of oak or some filtration. In the third stage it's bottled and it develops a completely different personality. This is the 'bouquet', a result of bottle age.

CAPSULE This is one way to take your Panadol after too big a night. It's also the plastic or faux lead wrapper that adorns the top of the bottle. When the capsule is completely removed – rather than surgically circumcised the way it should be – the bottle is referred to as 'naked'.

DEPTH Another term describing how much fruit you can taste in your mouth. A red with plenty of depth has plenty of fruit flavour.

FINISH The taste a wine leaves you with – arguably the most important bit.

MOUSSE This is a fantastic word to describe all the frothy bubbles on the head of a glass of sparkling wine. If a wine's got good mousse then it's got plenty of persistent bubble – and it's creamy in texture too.

NEBBIOLO This is one of Italy's great red grapes. No grape seems to represent the feminine and the masculine quite as well as nebbiolo. It has amazingly powerful tannins and a really delicate perfume. When aged, it has a fragrance of both tar and roses. There's not much planted in Australia but the little bit in the King Valley in Victoria shows promise.

NEW WORLD Quite a silly colonial term used by the Brits when describing Australian, New Zealand and any other wine that's not European.

NOSE This is obviously the thing in the middle of your face but in wine language it refers to the aroma or bouquet of a wine.

OAK Oak was used historically to make barrels because it was easy to work. Now the flavours and feel oak gives to wine are an integral part of winemaking. Other woods have been tried but produce either leaky barrels or bad flavours. Oak flavour can be given to wine in other forms, like chips, and can come in a multitude of nationalities: French, American, German, Yugoslavian and even Russian.

SANGIOVESE Arguably Italy's most famous red variety, sangiovese is the main grape in the wines of Chianti. It is planted in small amounts in Australia.

Adjectives (or words to describe things with)

AGGRESSIVE A wine that assaults the nose, throat or another part of the anatomy. Not necessarily a negative term.

ALCOHOLIC Obvious really, when referring to an alcoholic drink like wine, but some alcohol pokes through in some wines more than others – hence this term.

BIG The effect in the mouth of a generous wine. As in rude stuff, it's mostly a good thing.

BRIARY This is a typical wine word. Not a common aroma but one often present in red wines and sometimes in whites. It's the smell of briar, which is leafy, vegetal and reminiscent of undergrowth.

BROAD For some reason breadth is not as revered in the wine world as length, and 'broad' is a pejorative term for a wine lacking in definition.

BUTTERY Normally applied to white wine, this is an adjective that applies to taste and texture and not saturated fats.

CLOYING The effect of too much sweetness in the mouth. It lingers like a sycophantic visitor overstaying his or her welcome.

CREAMY Obvious enough: the textural quality some wines have.

CRISP This refers to the acidity in wine, particularly white. A crisp chardonnay, for instance, will have a clean, fresh acid finish after you've swallowed. Crisp is the opposite to cloying.

DUMB A wine that does not exhibit much aroma. It's not speaking – at least not in an olfactory sense.

ELEGANT Stylish, subtle and not obvious – also a polite way of saying thin.

FAT (or FLABBY) This is wine that has too much fruit sweetness and alcohol and not enough acid. The wine might have plenty of flavour, but it can be an endurance test if you plan to drink more than a glass of it.

FLESHY A nice way of saying the wine has stacks of fruit. Chewy is another way of describing this, as is muscular.

HARD A wine with too much acid.

HERBAL The smells and flavours of herbs. Herbaceous is even better, if you're into wine words.

HOT A wine that tastes too alcoholic or heady. This term can also be applied to the young and unbelievably attractive new sales rep for a major wine company.

INTEGRATED A wine that's well stitched together; the fruit, acid, tannin and alcohol come together seamlessly.

JAMMY A wine that has overripe and cooked fruit flavours.

LONG Flavour that lasts and lingers. A 'long' wine is preferable to a short one. As in rude stuff, so in wine.

NON-VINTAGE These words, or the abbreviation NV, are normally used to describe sparkling wine that is a blend of different vintages. It can also be used as a derogatory term for someone who won't reveal their age.

ROUND A word that refers to the feel of a wine in your mouth. A round wine has no corners or sharp edges.

SMOOTH This refers to the absence of harsh tannins. A wine that glides down the throat without gripping cheeks and tongue is considered smooth.

SPICY Spicy is a wine word normally used when a wine person can't identify the spice in question. It can refer to the pepperiness in a cool-climate shiraz, to the green spices in a sauvignon blanc or to the cinnamon and nutmeg effect of French oak on pinot noir.

THIN An uncomplimentary term applied to wine that tastes a bit watery.

TOASTY An intriguing aroma that pops up in aged white wine. In everything from aged riesling and semillon to old champagne there can generally be found a hint of toastiness. It's quite a comforting aroma.

VANILLAN A common aroma in red wine is vanilla. No, vanilla beans are not chucked into the ferment; the flavour is derived from oak, and in particular American oak. The same effect can be seen in bourbon.

VOLATILE An adjective used to describe a drunken English soccer crowd after yet another defeat, or a wine that has been exposed to oxygen and is beginning to turn to vinegar. See the similarity? A tiny bit of volatility can be attractive – like tipsiness, smudgy make-up or messed-up hair. A lot can be disgusting.

Technical terms (or words to be purposely silly with)

ALDEHYDE Or more correctly, acetaldehyde. This is the aroma in older wine that smells a bit like nail-polish remover. Aldehydic is the smarty-pants adjective.

AMPELOGRAPHY This is the proper name for the science of identifying and classifying grape vines.

BOTRYTIS A mould that attacks grapes causing them to go all horrible and yucky, but that also enables them to concentrate certain flavours. It's (only) really useful in making sweet dessert whites.

EXTRACT An oft-heard wine word referring to the tannin, colour and flavour extracted from grape skins and/or oak. It's usually used poo-pooingly.

MALOLACTIC FERMENTATION Referred to by those in the know as 'malo', It is the process by which hard malic acid turns into softer lactic acid. It's a natural process in red wines and is used to soften acids in some whites – notably chardonnay.

OENOLOGIST This is a vague term. It can be used to describe a winemaker or just someone who drinks a lot of wine. For instance: Is he pissed? No, he's an oenologist . . .

ORGANOLEPSY The (quite ridiculous and very serious) analysis of food or wine by the use of the senses.

OXIDATION This is the effect of oxygen on wine. In small amounts it can be beneficial; in large amounts it turns the wine to vinegar.

PHENOLICS Phenols come from grape skins and seeds. They give white wine gruffness just like tannins (q.v.) do red. Tannins in red are good but phenolics in white are generally bad, particularly when there are too many of them.

SULPHUR (SO_2) Used for thousands of years for the preservation of wine, sulphur dioxide, a.k.a. Preservative 220, is present at some level in any decent wine. Basically, it stops wine from going off. It inhibits oxidisation, discolouring and unwanted bacteria and yeasts. In good Australian wines it's at very low levels, like 30 parts per million and often a lot less. Some people are more sensitive to it than others. Sweet wines contain the most, white wine has more than red wine, and pinot noir generally contains a bit more than shiraz and cabernet sauvignon.

TANNIN Tannin is to red wine what the skeleton is to vertebrates. It's the structure the whole thing hangs off. It comes from the grape skins, pips, stems and the oak. It provides texture and finish. It's crucial to red wine and in most cases the amount of tannin can be controlled by the winemaker (out of a bag marked 'tannin'). It is often overdone.

TERROIR (pronounced tare-wah) A French word that has snuck into the language because it sounds poncy and knowledgeable and represents a vague concept for which there's no word in English. It refers to the way one particular chunk of land can give an indefinable character to a wine. There are scientific reasons for such things but *terroir* sounds so much more romantic.

VARIETAL An uninspired wine word that simply means that a wine tastes like the grape variety it is made from.

ULLAGE A very handy word that refers to the space between the wine and the cork. In an old bottle no ullage is seen as a good thing because the cork hasn't leaked.

Jargon (or words and phrases needed in order to play with wine bores and sommeliers)

ARTIFACT Top-drawer tossy wine word referring to flavours that the winemaker (as opposed to nature) has determinedly given to the wine – oak smells and flavours are an example. 'This chardonnay shows a lot of artifact.'

CHARACTER This is a wonderful word to use when you are not really sure what is going on in the glass: 'It has an interesting sort of laundromat character, don't you think?' The key word is often then turned into an adjective by banging a 'y' on the end: laundromatty, kennelly, finessy, eucalyptusy, oilyly . . . Use this ad nauseum, no worries.

CORK TAINT Often misunderstood, this is one of the big issues in wine. Cork is susceptible to various mould infections. The mould subsequently contaminates the wine, making it smell like wet cardboard and wet dogs. The wine also tastes pretty flat and inert. To normal humans who don't know about cork taint, this condition simply equates to 'bad wine'. This is why winemakers hate cork taint, and why some producers use plastic corks, or screw caps. Bored wine connoisseurs find cork taint most amusing and jump out of their chair when they come across such a wine, shouting 'Corked!' with all the gusto of a victorious bingo player. Wine is, indeed, a very strange drug.

DECANTING This is the process of pouring an entire bottle of wine into a jug or a special decanter before pouring it into the glasses. Decanting helps a wine – particularly young red wines – to open up a little; they can often be a bit shy, and this process helps. Don't be afraid once you've decanted to swish the wine around in the jug a little – in fact, be quite brutal. Get a good-looking woman to do this for you, and all the blokes in the room will go spare, no worries . . .

FUNCTIONAL ALCOHOL WARMTH A clever way to say that you can taste the alcohol in the wine and, while it is high, it's acceptable.

LIFTED When a wine's smell is strong but the exact descriptor eludes you, say 'Yes, quite lifted, isn't it?'

LOOK (or SEEN) 'Have you seen the new Château Mates-Maison Shiraz?' To look at or to have seen a wine is to have tasted it. Wine people do not taste – they look and see. A la-di-da wine that does not taste very good is said to be 'Not showing very well . . .'.

M.W. Abbreviation of Master of Wine. An 'Em-Double-You' is a person who knows a lot about wine as they have passed a test about wine held by the Institute of Masters of Wine. Traditionally M.W.s wore tweed and drank a lot of brandy, but now they are very serious young insects indeed . . .

OAK REGIME This is very hard to use without breaking into laughter. An oak regime is the type of oak a winemaker uses and the way he or she uses it. It's a much smarter way of saying 'oak'.

OVERDELIVERY Marketing tosser's highest praise: 'It overdelivers at this price point!', i.e. the wine is good value.

PALATE TRAVEL We are very proud of this term because we think we invented it. It refers to the way a wine moves through your mouth – if, indeed, you are one of those people who use your mouth when tasting wine. There's good P.T. and bad P.T.

PALATE WEIGHT How much the wine weighs in your mouth. This is very easy to assess as mouths were originally designed by God to weigh things.

PHILOSOPHY A word that appears regularly on back labels referring to the winemaker's thought process. It is a misnomer. Philosophy is not part of winemaking curriculum and most winemakers think John Stuart Mill is an English Master of Wine.

SMART A smart wine is a wine of agreed high quality, regardless of the actual quality of the wine. High praise, but best used begrudgingly: 'Quite smart . . .'

TYPICITY This means the wine is typical of the place or grape it has come from. Ideally, you use this word when you don't actually know what the typicity really is.

INDEX

Sherry

La Gitana Manzanilla	171
'La Goya' Manzanilla	170

Sparkling

Brown Brothers Patricia Pinot Noir Chardonnay Brut 1997	141
Brown Brothers Pinot Noir & Chardonnay	6
Orlando Trilogy Cuvée Brut	43
Pirie 1998	78
Yarra Burn Pinot Noir Chardonnay Pinot Meunier 2000	7
Yarrabank Cuvée 1998	142

Imported Sparkling

Bollinger Champagne Special Cuvée	79
Carpenè Malvolti Prosecco di Conegliano	172
Devaux Grande Reserve Champagne	111
Lanson Black Label Champagne	143

Riesling

Brown Brothers Riesling 2002	8
Knights Granite Hills Riesling 2002	144
Leasingham Bastion Riesling 2002	46
Leasingham Bin 7 Riesling 2002	80
Leo Buring Clare Valley Riesling 2002	112
Jacob's Creek Reserve Riesling 2001	81
Jacob's Creek Riesling 2002	44
Miranda High Country Riesling 2002	9
Lindemans Bin 75 Riesling 2002	45
Orlando Steingarten Riesling 2001	113
Taylors Riesling 2002	11
Wynns Coonawarra Riesling 2002	10

Semillon

Littles Reserve Semillon 2001	145
McWilliams Elizabeth Semillon 1999	83
Peter Lehmann Reserve Semillon 1998	114
Poet's Corner Henry Lawson Semillon 2001	13
Rosemount Diamond Label Semillon 2002	48
Rosemount Show Reserve Semillon 2002	84
Tyrrell's Lost Block Semillon 2002	12
Tyrrell's Old Winery Semillon 2002	47

Sauvignon Blanc

Craggy Range Sauvignon Blanc 2002	149
Houghton Pemberton Sauvignon Blanc 2002	115
Miranda High Country Sauvignon Blanc 2002	14
Oyster Bay Sauvignon Blanc 2002	15
Palandri Sauvignon Blanc 2002	146
Shadowfax Adelaide Hills Sauvignon Blanc 2002	147
Starvedog Lane Sauvignon Blanc 2002	82
Vavasour Sauvignon Blanc 2002	148

Semillon/Sauvignon Blanc Blends

Hazard Hill Semillon Sauvignon Blanc 2002	51
Houghton Semillon Sauvignon Blanc 2002	50
Jacob's Creek Semillon Sauvignon Blanc 2002	49

Chardonnay

Dromana Estate Reserve Chardonnay 2001	119
Gembrook Hill Chardonnay 2001	150
Gramp's Barossa Chardonnay 2001	20
Houghton Chardonnay 2002	56
Howard Park Chardonnay 2001	86
Isabel Estate Chardonnay 2001	117
Jacob's Creek Limited Release Chardonnay 2002	85

Koonunga Hill Chardonnay 2002	16
Miranda High Country Chardonnay 2002	17
Moondah Brook Chardonnay 2002	19
Pegasus Bay Chardonnay 2001	118
Pipers Brook Reserve Chardonnay 2000	77
Shaw and Smith M3 Chardonnay 2001	87
Stonier Chardonnay 2002	116
Tin Cows Chardonnay 2001	151
Trinity Hill Shepherds Croft Chardonnay 2001	152
Tyrrell's Vat 47 Chardonnay 2001	90
Wirra Wirra Adelaide Hills Chardonnay 2002	88
Wynns Coonawarra Chardonnay 2002	18
Yering Station Chardonnay 2001	89

Blended Whites

Encounter Bay Classic Dry White 2001	53
Houghton White Burgundy 2002	52
Penfolds Rawson's Retreat Semillon Chardonnay 2002	55

Other Whites

Tahbilk Marsanne 2002	54
Tamar Ridge Pinot Gris 2002	120

Imported Whites

William Fevre Petit Chablis 2001	174
Umani Ronchi Villa Bianchi Verdicchio Dei Castelli di Jesi 2001	173

Rosé

Pizzini Rosetta 2002	121

Pinot Noir

De Bortoli Gulf Station Pinot Noir 2001	21
De Bortoli Windy Peak Pinot Noir 2001	57
De Bortoli Yarra Valley Pinot Noir 2000	92
Meadowbank Henry James Pinot Noir 2001	122
Meadowbank Pinot Noir 2002	153
Ninth Island Pinot Noir 2002	22
Pegasus Bay Pinot Noir 2001	154
Pipers Brook Estate 2002	91
Tarrawarra Pinot Noir 2001	123

Merlot

Lindemans Cawarra Merlot 2002	61
Moondah Brook Merlot 2001	23
Penfolds Rawson's Retreat Merlot 2002	63
Yalumba Merlot 2002	62

Shiraz

Brown Brothers Shiraz 2001	93
Cape Mentelle Shiraz 2001	95
Cascabel Fleurieu Shiraz 2001	127
Cheviot Bridge Shiraz 2001	157
d'Arenberg Laughing Magpie Shiraz/ Viognier 2002	124
Ferngrove Dragon Shiraz 2001	159
Firefly Shiraz 2002	64
Hardys Tintara Shiraz 1999	130
Howard Park Scotsdale Shiraz 2001	161
Jane Brook Back Block Shiraz 2001	156
Kangarilla Road Shiraz 2001	128
Knappstein Shiraz 2001	31
Metala Black Label Shiraz 2000	131
Mitchelton Central Victoria Shiraz 2001	98
Mount Langi Ghiran Cliff Edge Shiraz 2001	96
Redman Coonawarra Shiraz 2001	94
Rosemount Hill of Gold Shiraz 2001	30
Scorpo Mornington Peninsula Shiraz 2001	158
Shadowfax McLaren Vale Shiraz 2001	160
St Hallett Faith Shiraz 2001	129
Stepping Stone Padthaway Shiraz 2001	67
Tatachilla Breakneck Creek Shiraz 2002	68
Taylors Shiraz 2001	32
Tyrrell's Old Winery Shiraz 2001	66
Water Wheel Bendigo Shiraz 2001	35

Wynns Coonawarrra Shiraz 2001	29	Water Wheel Memsie 2002	5
Yalumba Galway Shiraz 2001	65	Wirra Wirra Church Block 2001	126
Yering Station Reserve Shiraz 2001	97		

Cabernet Sauvigon

Other Reds

		Gary Crittenden 'i' Nebbiolo 2000	162
Grant Burge Cameron Vale Cabernet		Pizzini Sangiovese 2002	110
Sauvignon 2001	100	Yalumba Barossa Bush Vine Grenache 2000	27
Houghton Rockwall Cabernet Sauvignon 2001	28		
Mildara Coonawarra Cabernet Sauvignon 2000	102		

Imported Reds

Mitchelton Blackwood Park Cabernet		Château de Montfaucon Côtes du Rhône 2000	183
Sauvignon 2000	33	Château Villerambert Julien Minervois 2000	181
Penfolds Rawson's Retreat Cabernet		Felsina Berardenga Chianti Classico 2000	179
Sauvignon 2002	42	Guigal Côtes du Rhône 2000	182
Rymill Cabernet Sauvignon 1999	101	Riecine Chianti Classico 2000	180
Summerfield Cabernet 2001	163	Riparosso Montelpulciano d'Abruzzo	
Tahbilk Cabernet Sauvignon 2000	34	Illuminati 2000	175
		Speri Valpolicella Superiore 2000	177

Red Blends

		Valderiz Ribera del Duero 2000	178
Cascabel Tempranillo/Graciano 2001	140	Zenato Valpolicella Classico Superiore 1999	176
d'Arenberg Stump Jump Red 2002	25		

Sparkling Reds

Grant Burge The Holy Trinity Grenache Shiraz			
Mourvèdre 2000	99	Seaview Sparkling Shiraz	70
Jacob's Creek Grenache Shiraz 2002	58		

Sweet Whites

Leasingham Bastion Shiraz Cabernet 2001	69		
Mad Fish Premium Red 2001	26	Pegasus Bay Riesling 2002	132
Peter Lehmann Shiraz Grenache 2002	60	Margan Botrytis Semillon 2002	133
Rosemount Diamond Label Grenache		Mitchelton Blackwood Park Botrytis	
Shiraz 2002	59	Riesling 2002	103
Shadowfax K Road 2001	155		

Fortified

Shadow's Run Cabernet Shiraz 2001	24		
St Hallett Gamekeeper's Reserve 2002	125	Penfolds Club Reserve Tawny Port Bin 421	71

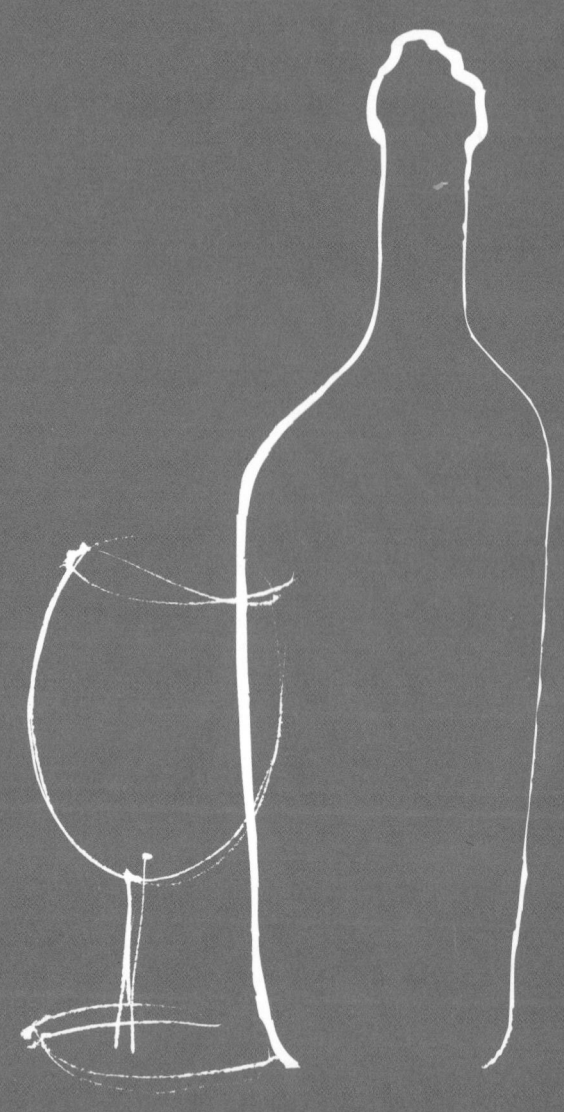